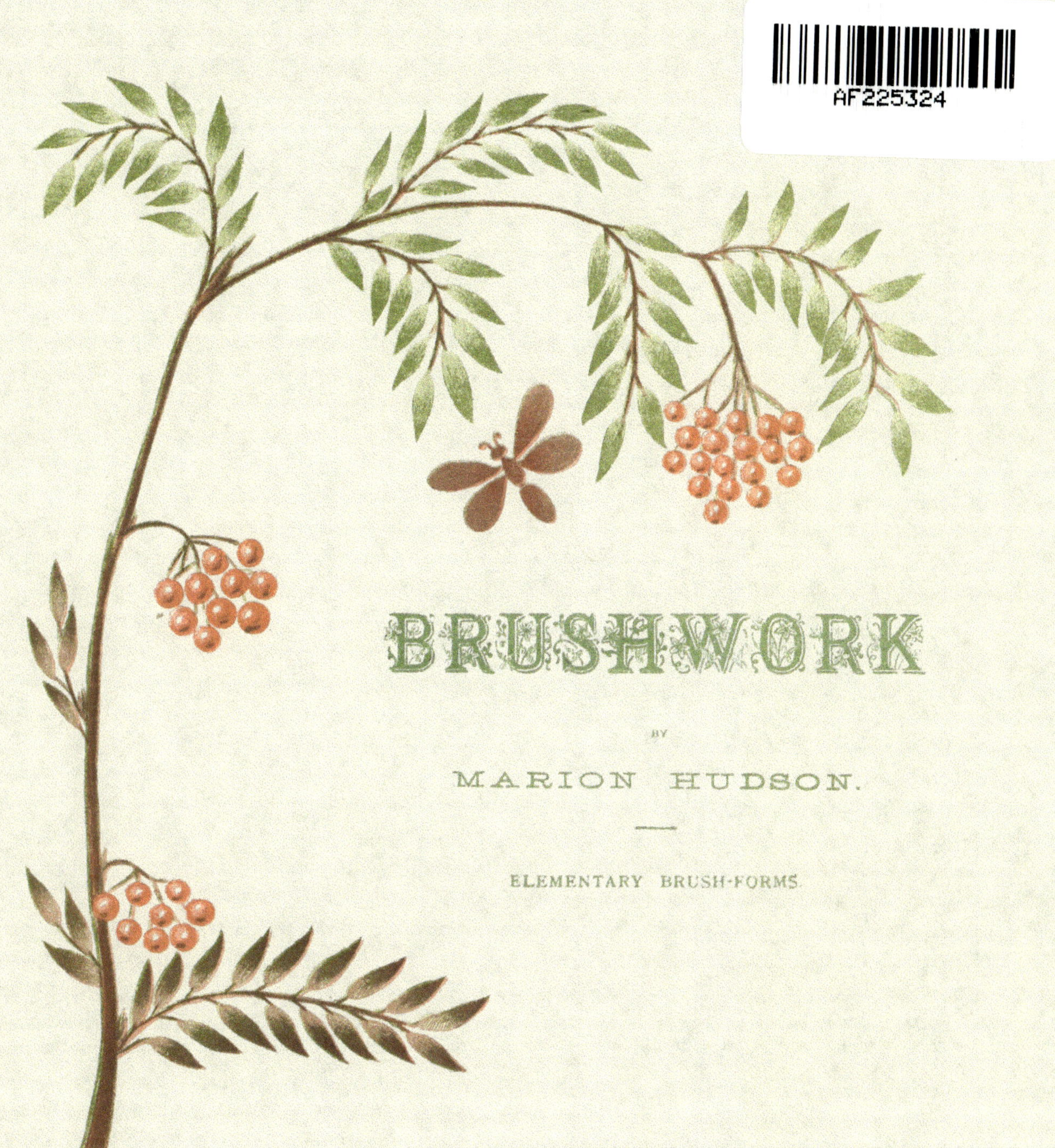

# BRUSHWORK

BY

## MARION HUDSON.

—

ELEMENTARY BRUSH-FORMS.

This edition published 2019
By Living Book Press



ISBN: 978-1-925729-94-8

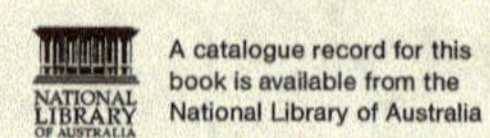
A catalogue record for this
book is available from the
National Library of Australia

# PREFACE.

THE following lessons in Brushwork are an attempt to show, by a series of typical lessons, how the subject may be taught to large classes in elementary schools.

Most of the lessons have been successfully given to such classes, and the difficulties are found to be greatly lessened by the observance of a few simple rules.

I have to gratefully express my indebtedness to my old friend and master, Mr. E. Cooke, to whom we owe the original idea of Brushwork as a means of education, for his kindness in looking through the sheets, and for giving me the benefit of his criticism.

# INTRODUCTION.

**AIMS.**—Brushwork as a means of education is intended to train the power of observation by means of the eye and the hand ; to give a knowledge of colour, form, and number, especially of familiar natural objects, such as flowers, birds, insects, etc., etc.; to develop originality and the power of imagination.

The elementary Brush-forms may be used either simply (Lessons 1 to 17), or they may be combined to represent natural objects, such as flowers, animals, insects, birds, etc. (Lessons 8, 12, 14, etc.) The object of the following lessons is not to provide copies to be used in schools, but merely to show the various ways in which the Brush-forms may be used. The lessons might easily be multiplied, so as to cover the various seasons of the year, but this is neither necessary nor desirable.

**PRINCIPLES.**—In order that the work may be of real educational value it is absolutely necessary:—

(*a*) That the teacher should not work from copies of any kind, but should discover suitable natural forms, and use these in his own way as the subject matter for each lesson.

(*b*) Each lesson should be adapted to the capacities of the scholars, their power to appreciate form and colour, and their ability to represent these.

(*c*) The object chosen for representation should be suited to the time of year.

(*d*) The Brushwork lesson should be connected, as far as possible, with the other lessons of the school, especially with the nature or object lessons.

In cases where a third colour must be used, it will be found sufficient to mix it in one or two extra pans and pass these round the class towards the end of the lesson.

In conclusion, I beg teachers not to be discouraged if in some cases the early results appear to be very much like smudges. It is natural that the first attempts of the child should appear to be clumsy, but care, time, and patience on the part of teacher and taught, will be certain to bring better results.

**METHOD.** — I have found the following points to be of importance in teaching the subject:—

(*a*) The object chosen should be seen and examined by each of the scholars. If an animal or insect form be selected, a good picture, or, preferably, a drawing prepared beforehand by the teacher, should be exhibited. The use of dead creatures is always undesirable.

(*b*) To draw from the children by questions the main characteristics of the object, avoiding too much detail, and, if possible, to make these more emphatic and graphic by means of a simple tale.

(*c*) Always to work with the children step by step, and as far as possible, to get from them suggestions for the forms and designs. These latter may be made so simple that the most elementary class can suggest them under the guidance of a good teacher.

(*d*) To so prepare the lesson beforehand as to ensure accuracy of form and symmetry in the design.

**COLOUR.**— Only six colours are used in these lessons, viz.:—
1.— Carmine;
2.— Light red;
3.— Indigo;
4.— Cobalt;
5.— Gamboge;
6.— Pale Chrome.

NOTE—Coloured inks have been successfully used as a substitute for some of the water colours.

In almost every case not more than two colours are required for each lesson in this series.

For the sake of simplicity it is necessary to make the leaves either of a bluish or yellowish green, according to which seems to be the prevailing tint.. All the greens necessary can be made by different combinations of the above blues and yellows.

The flowers should be made first in all cases, and the same brush may be used for the green without washing, as a slight tint of the flower colour usually improves the green.

What appear to be brown stalks are in all cases got by making the stalks first with the colour of the flower or berry, and then painting them over with green when quite dry (as in Lessons 6, 20, 22, 26).

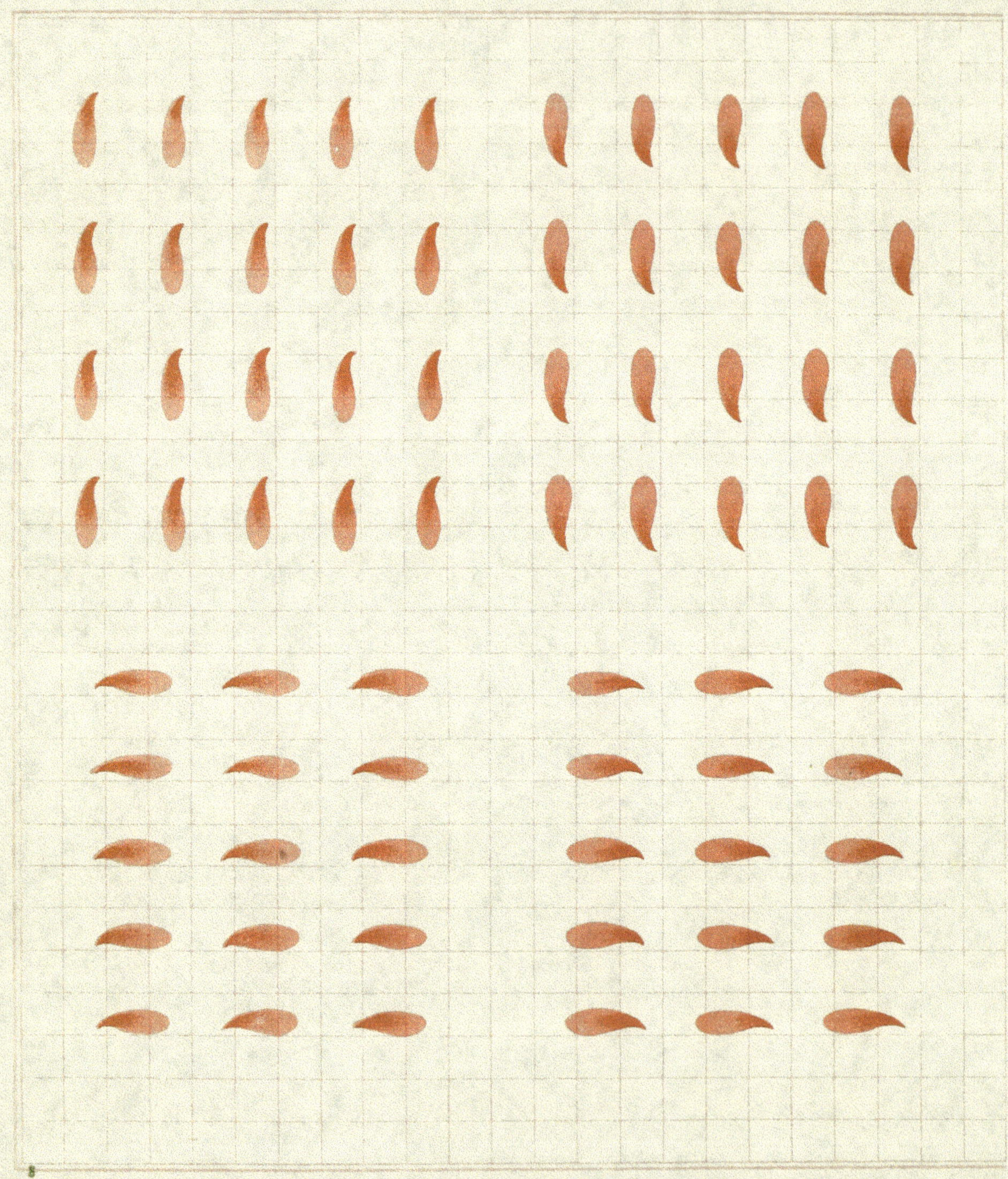

### No. 1 MODEL LESSON.

**BRUSH DRILL—** Take the brush in the right hand; discuss its two ends.
Point upwards;
" downwards;
" to the left-hand side;
" to the right-band side.

Lay the dry brush on the chequers in four directions, and measure the length of the brush. It should cover two chequers.

**BRUSH-FORMS.—** Fill the brush with colour, and lay it on the chequers in the first a position, viz. : pointing upwards, and raise it again without moving it on the paper. The result is a picture of the brush, or *Brush-form*.

Continue these until made correctly.

Proceed in the same way to teach the other three directions.

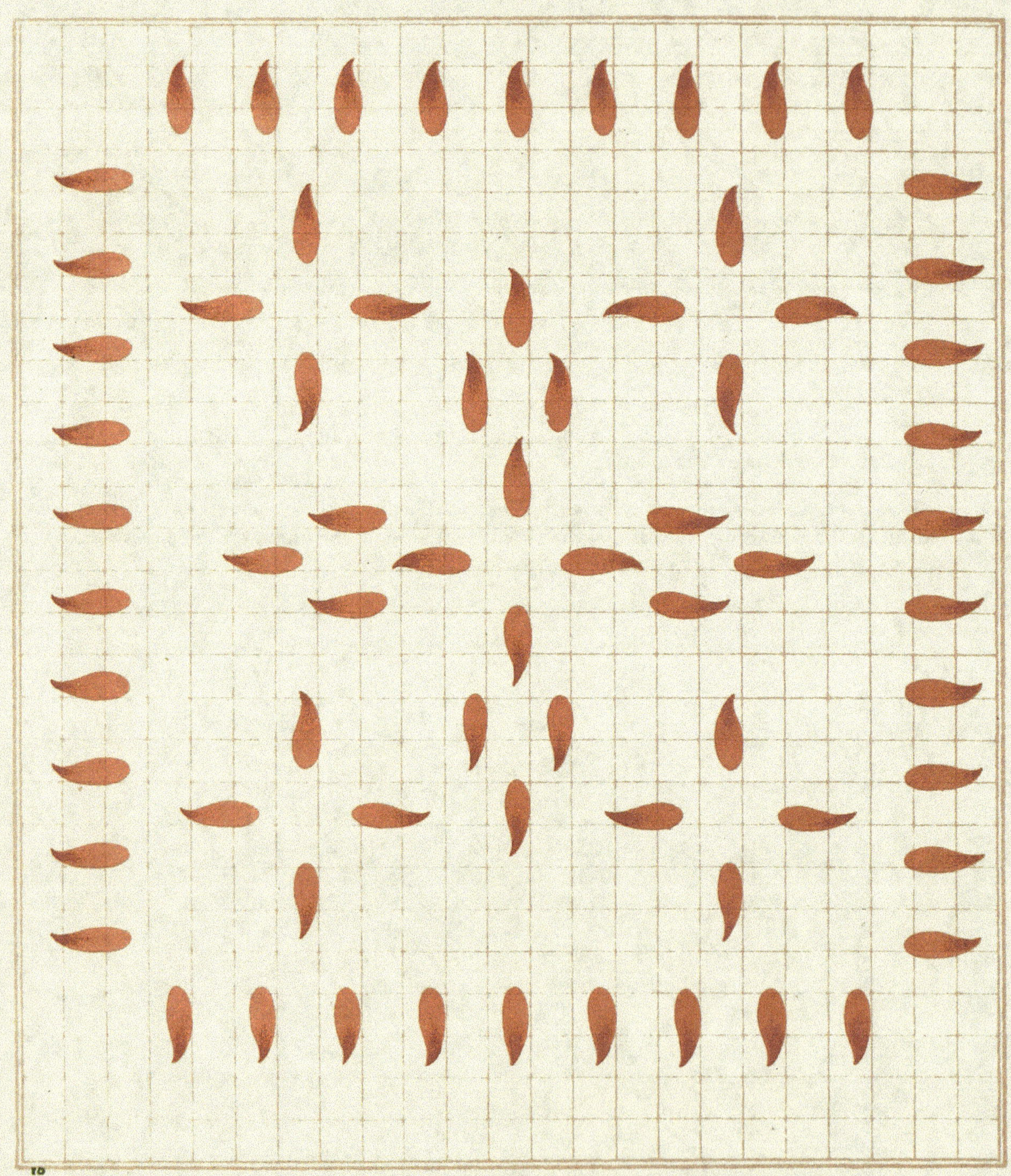

**No. 2 PATTERN.**

Find the centre of the paper by counting chequers; make border first; and fill in centre to suit size of paper, in a similar way to example given.

N.B.— Care must be taken that the brush is used in the four directions in making the pattern.

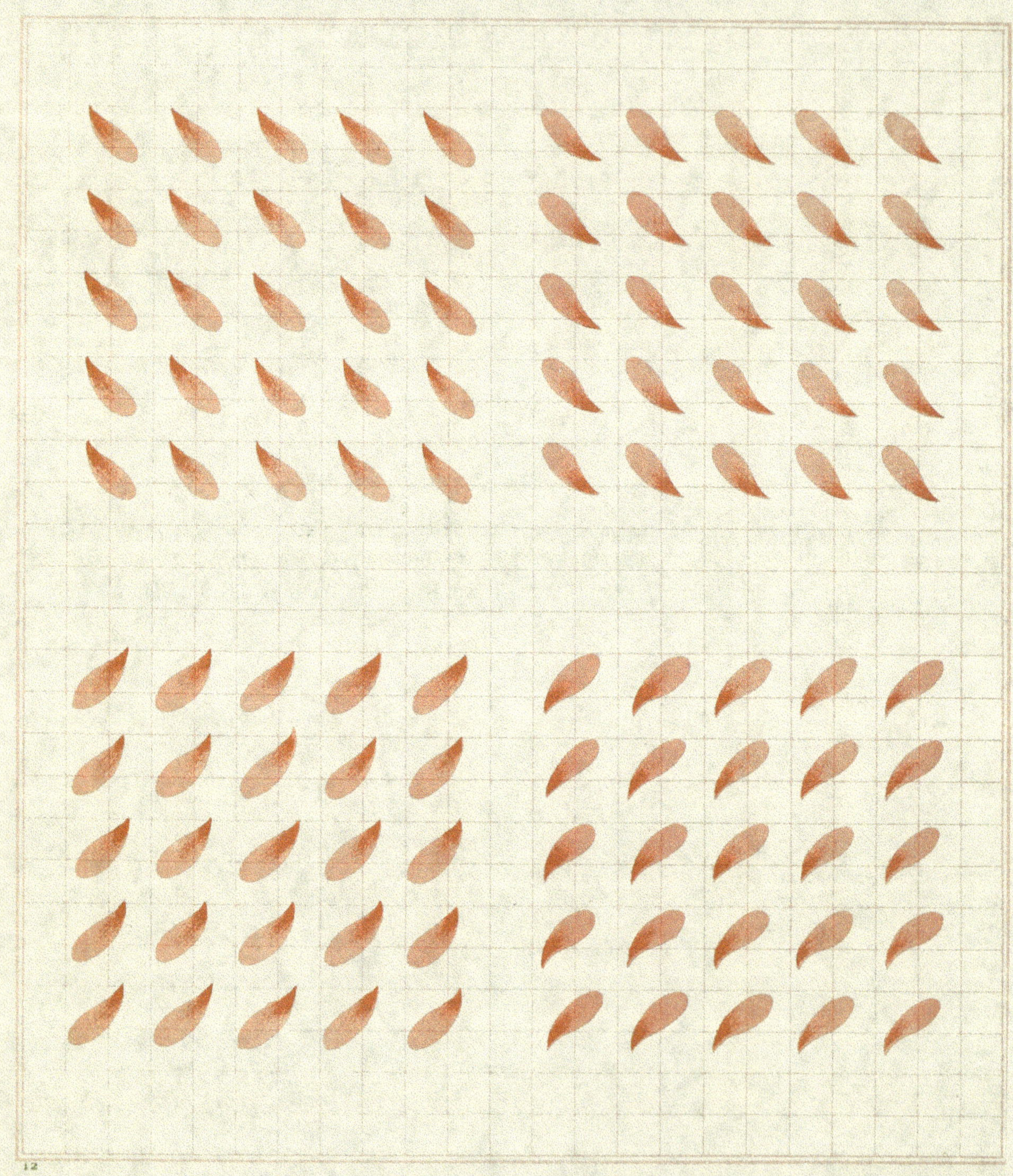

## LESSON 3.

**BRUSH DRILL.—** Teach the drill in four oblique directions. Repeat it on books, the brush forming the diagonal of large square containing four small squares.

Fill the brush with colour, and proceed as before.

Nos. 4 and 5 Patterns made with Brush-forms in the same way as No. 2 Lesson.

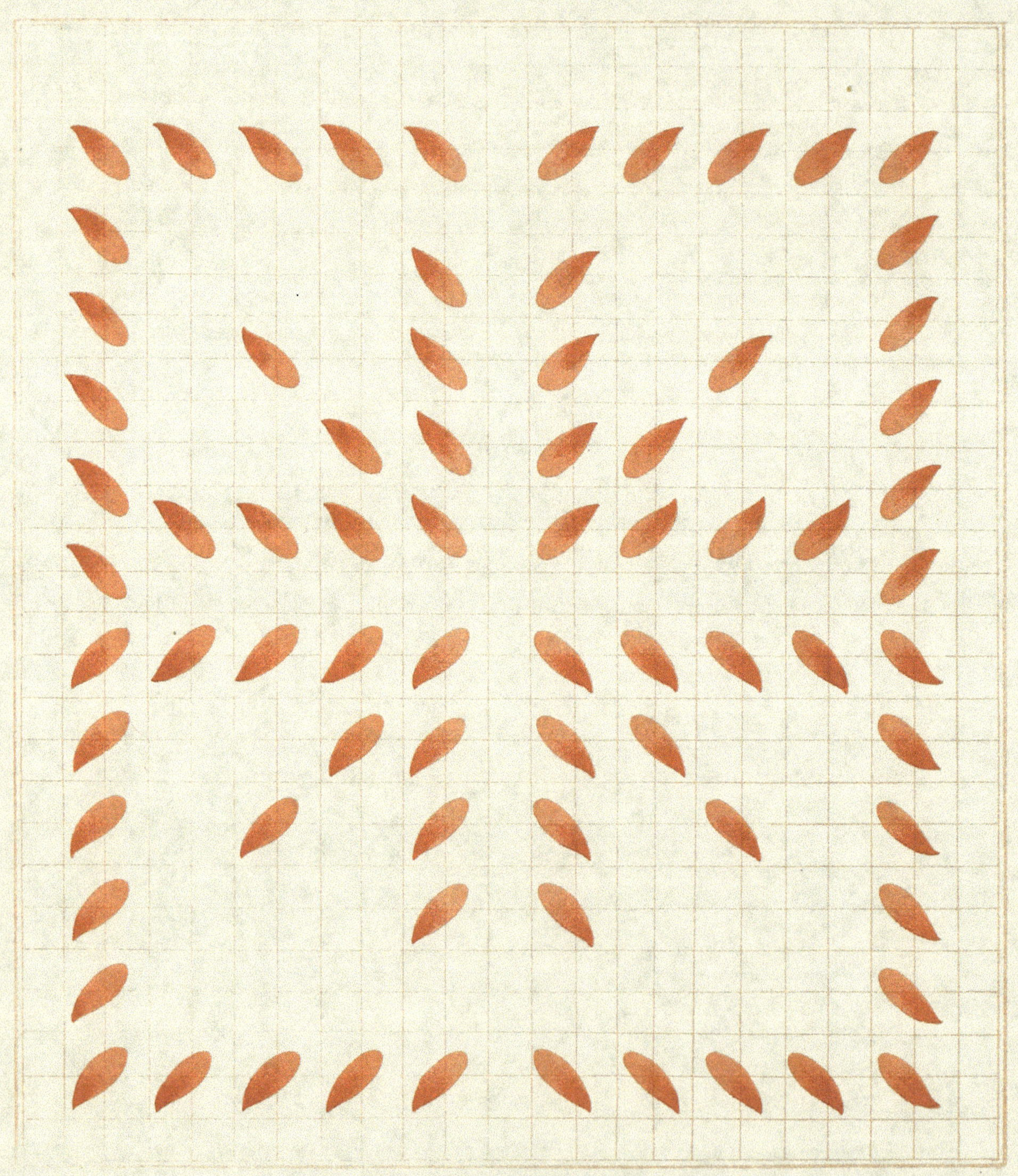

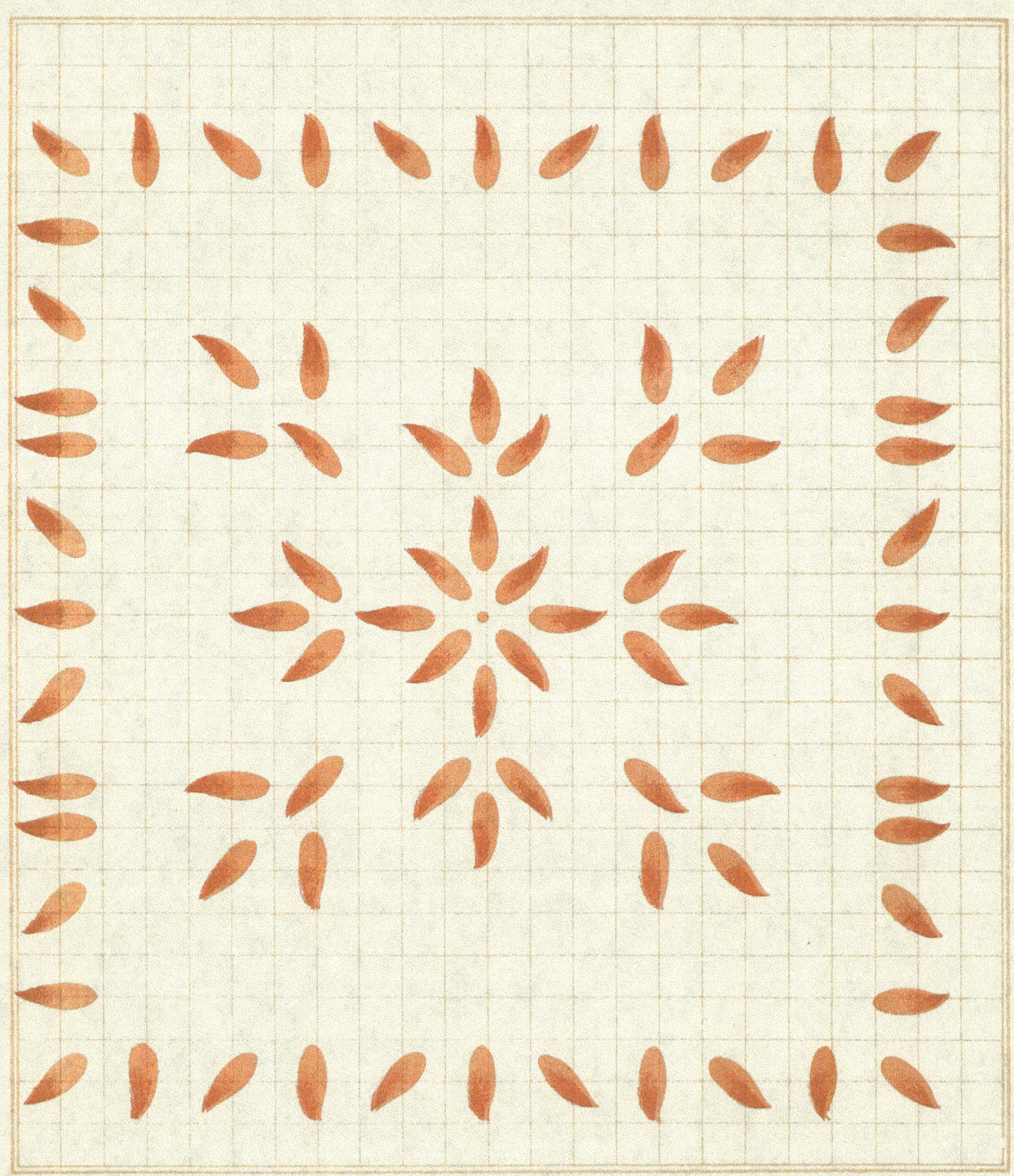

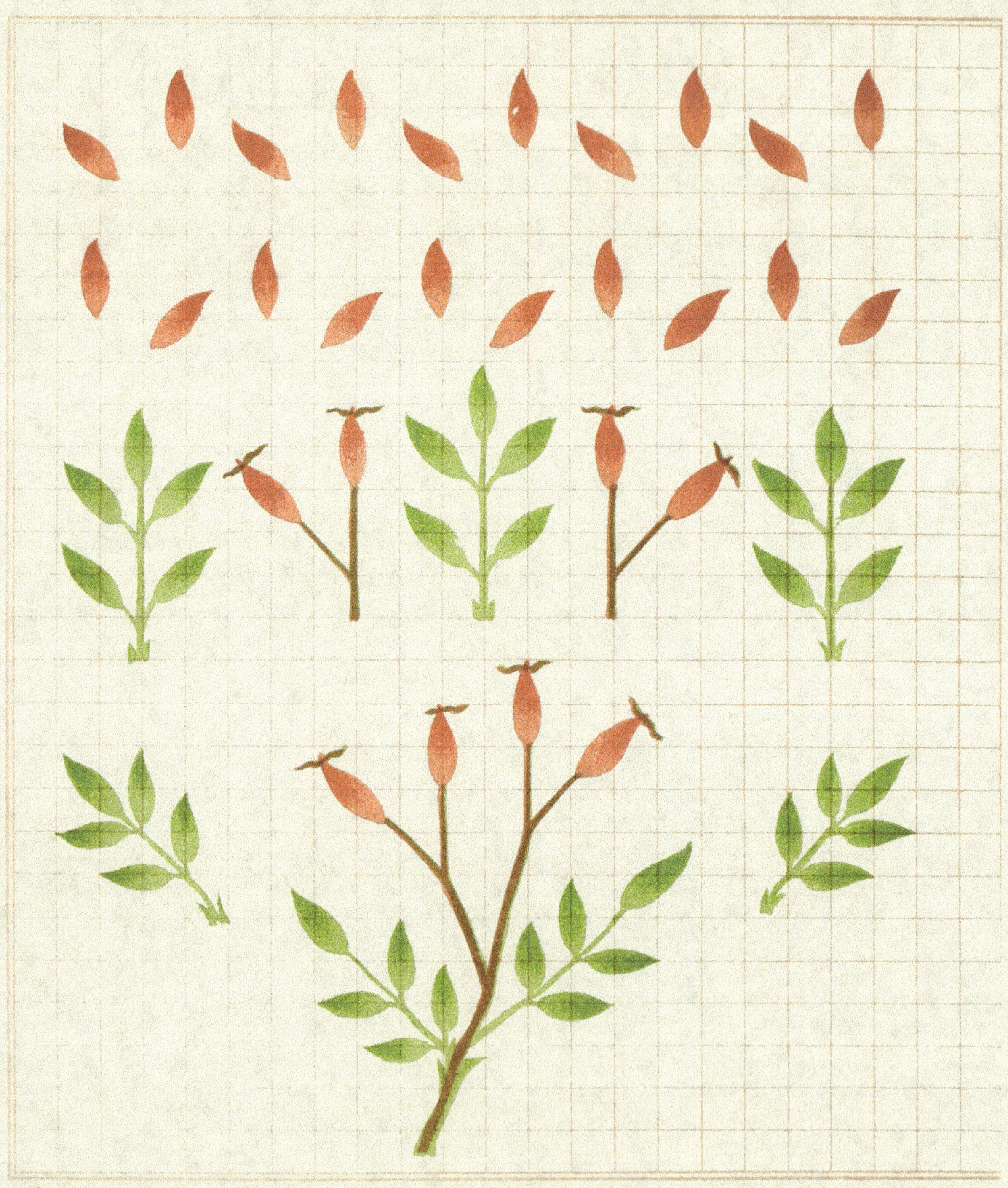

### No. 6 MODEL LESSON.

1.— Tell a simple tale of autumn time, introducing country lanes with hips on the hedges. Have a bunch of hips to show, and, if possible, distribute amongst the children.

Let the children thoroughly examine the berries and leaves, and note the number, arrangement, colour, etc., viz.:—

That the berries generally go in pairs, though there may be several pairs close together on the main stalk.

That the little leaflets forming the leaves are opposite, but the leaves themselves grow alternately on the stalk.

That the hips have little brown horns at the top, and what they are, what once grew there, and what is inside the hip, etc.

2.— With the red colour make the Brush-forms on the chequers from the teacher's dictation, thus—

Count the margin and four chequers from the edge of the page, and miss the margin at the top. Make one hip, with point of brush upwards.
From the bottom of this hip, count two chequers towards the edge, and make one hip across, and so on.
The leaves to be dictated in the same manner. It is necessary to be careful that the Brush-forms are placed on the chequers indicated, or the character of the growth will be lost.

Add stalks and calyx with the same colour, using point of brush.

3.— Free the brush as far as possible from the red colour, without washing it—take green, and make the leaves in the same manner. With the point of the brush, put green over the red of the calvx and stalks.

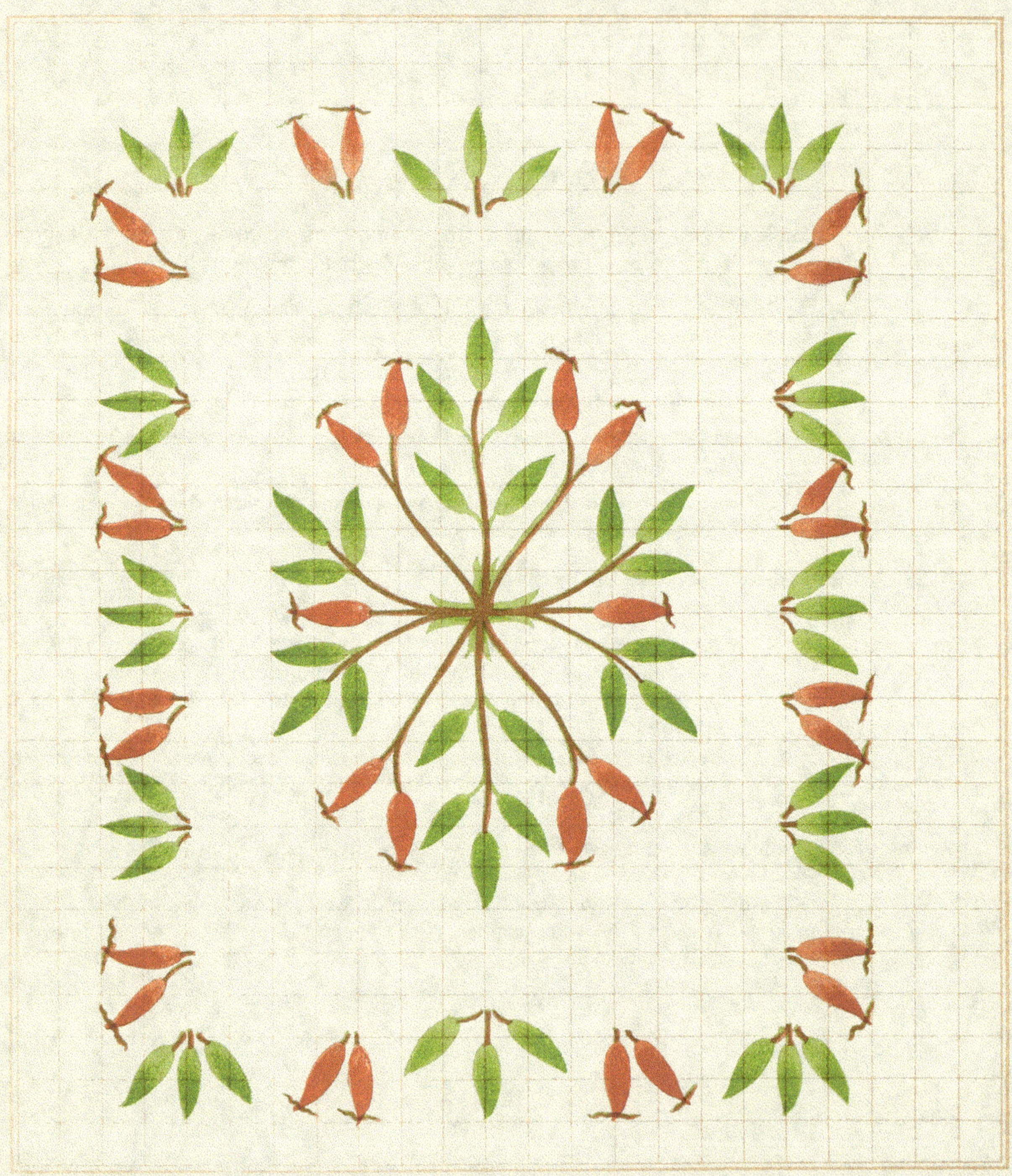

20

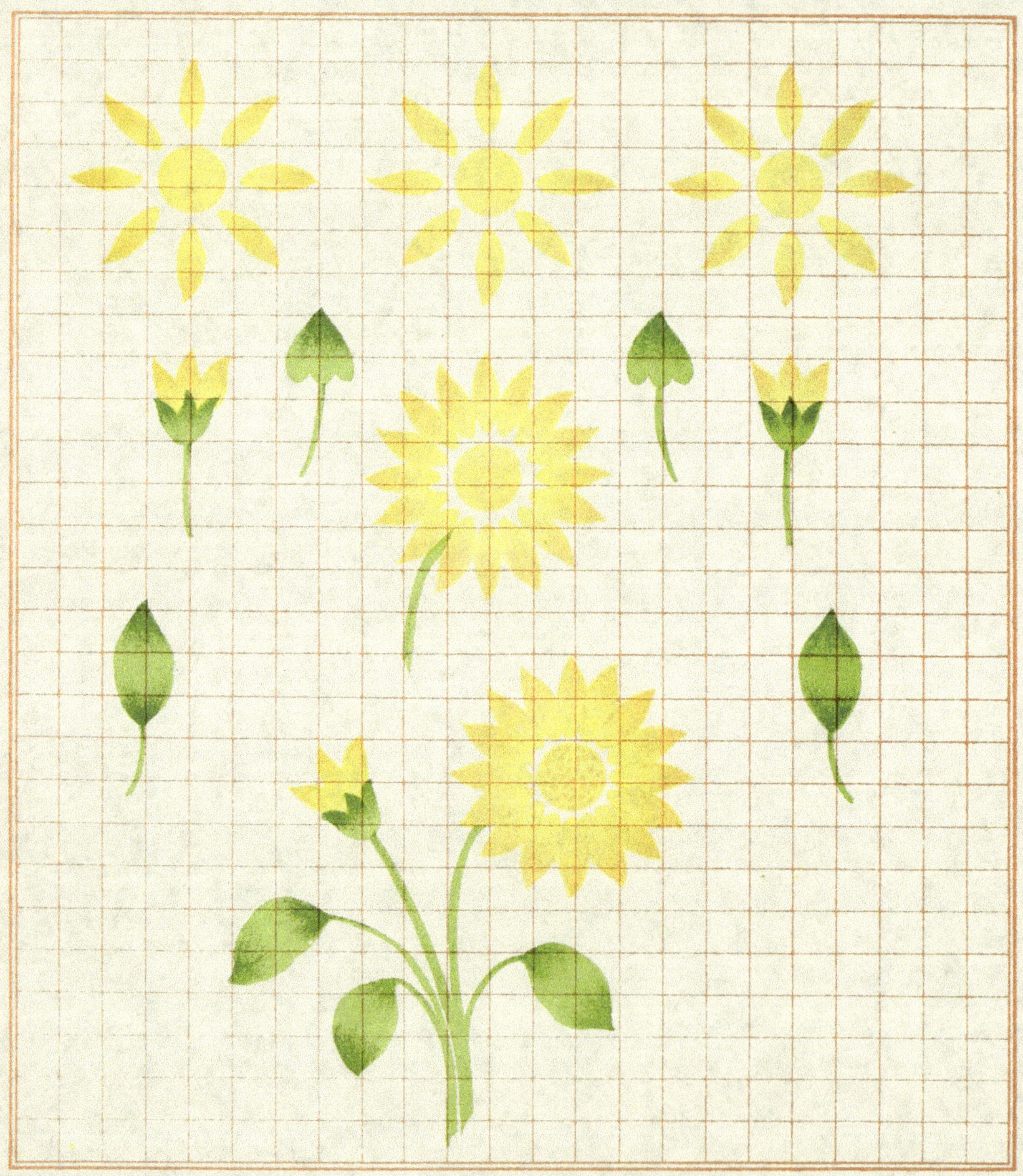

**LESSON 8.**

In the yellow dahlia the star form is made with the previous Brush-forms, leaving a space of two chequers for the centre. When dry, add one Brush-form between each pair in the star, and make irregular spots on the disc with the point of the brush.

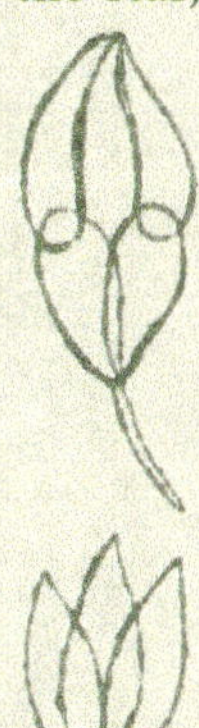

To make the leaves, place three Brush forms overlapping, having the point of the brush on the same spot. Add a stalk. Reverse the brush and place one Brush-form on each side of, and touching the stalk. Buds and calyx are made by overlapping in the same way, with the brush pointing upwards.

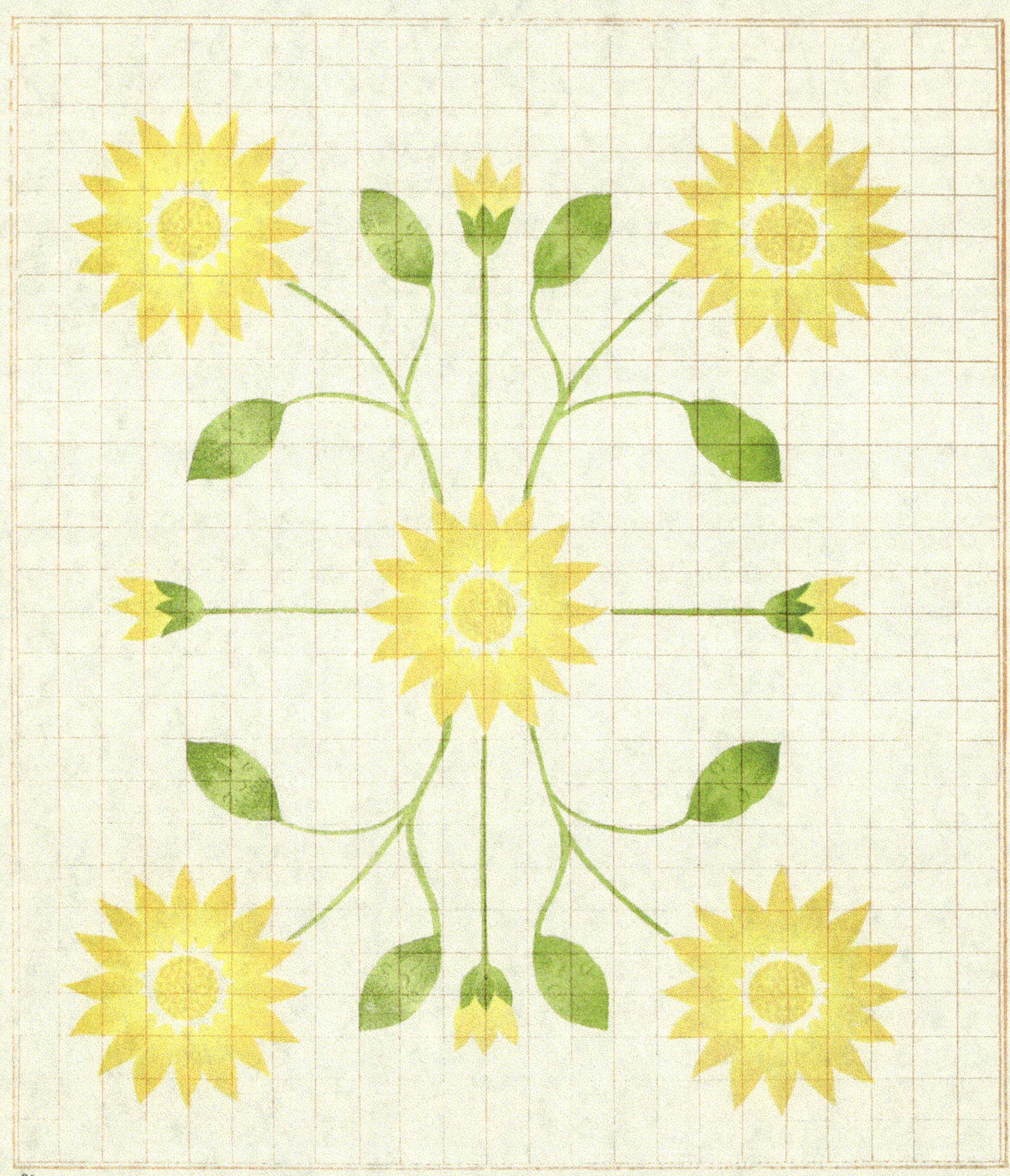

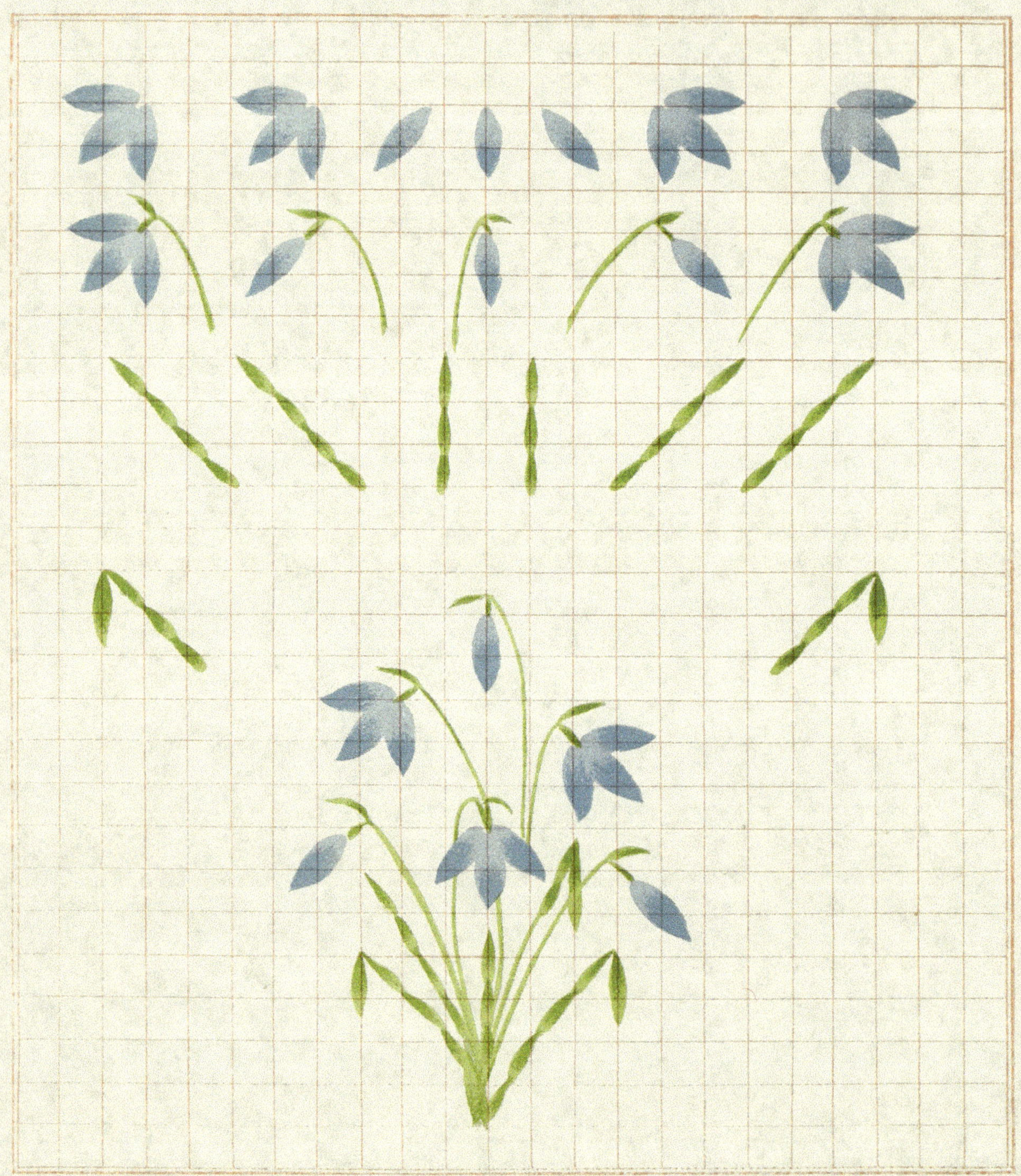

**LESSON 10.**

The Scylla is made with three overlapping Brush-forms, making a right angle.

The leaves should be made by touching the brush very lightly on the paper but when the children have learnt the length and direction required, they may make them in strokes, as in the following design.

Note the little sheath instead of a calyx, and get the children to give prettier examples.

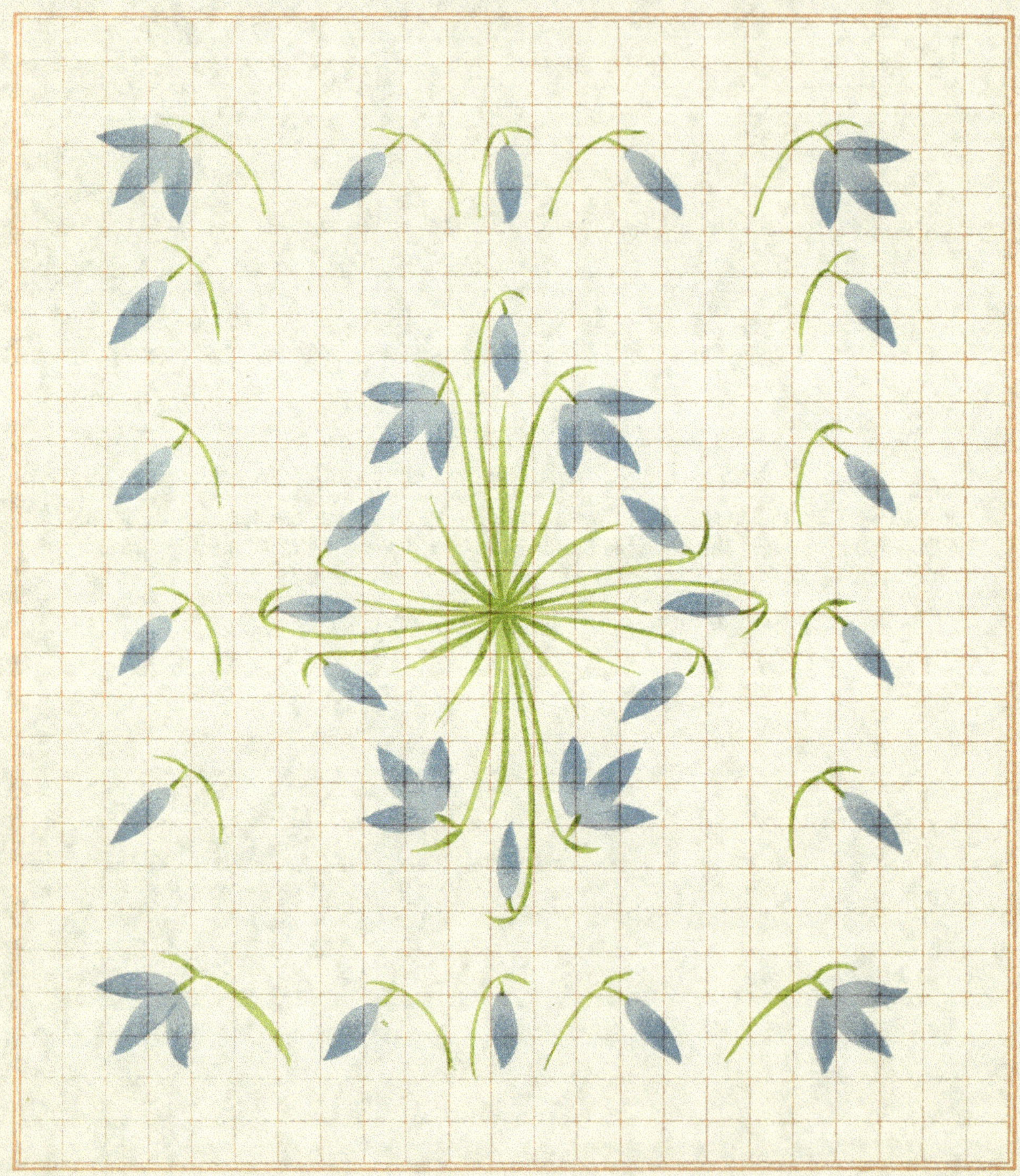

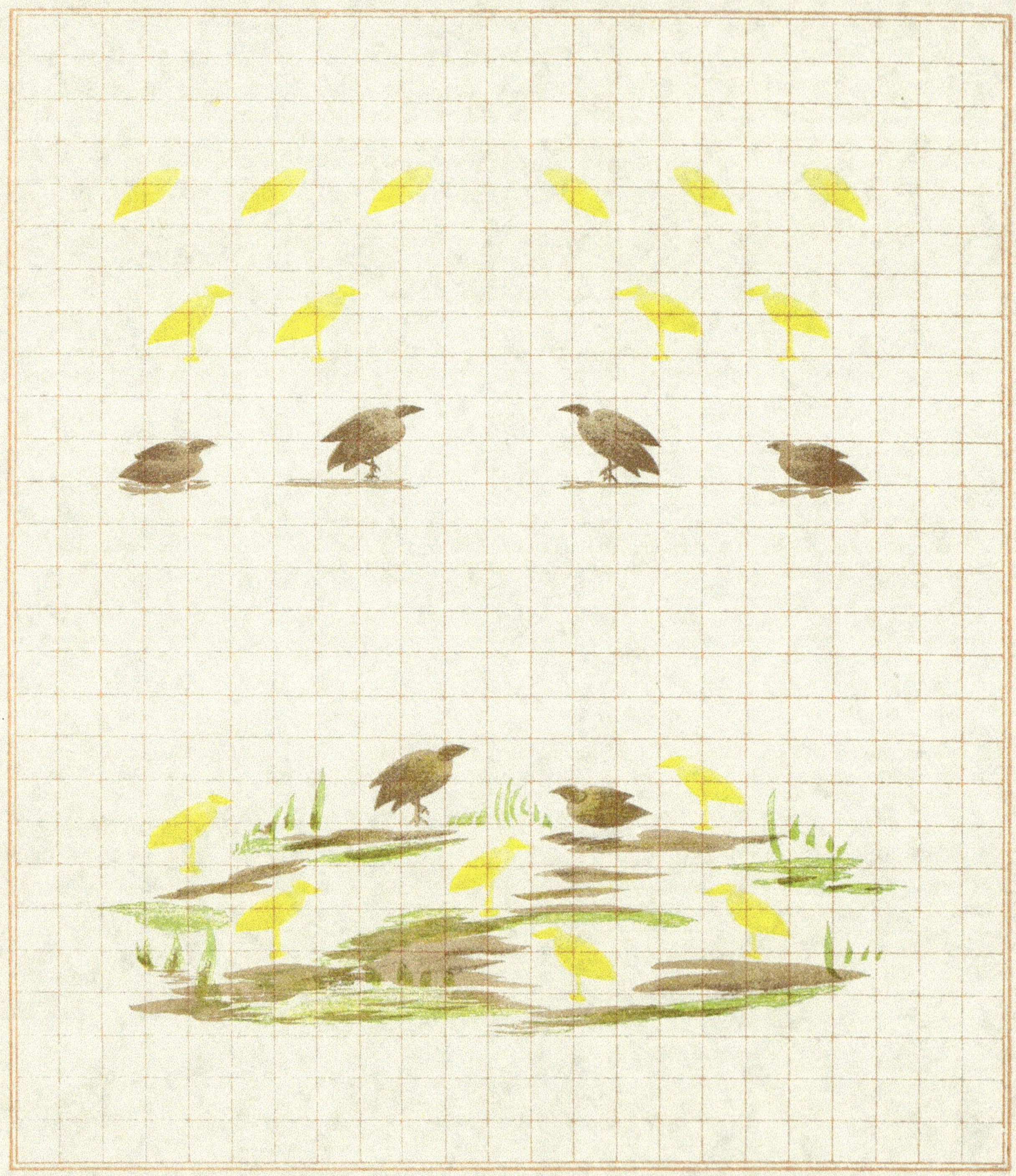

**LESSON 12.**

The chicks are made with one oblique Brush-form, with a touch of the point of the brush for the head.

The larger chickens, by a combination of three forms for the body, and the same touch for the head.

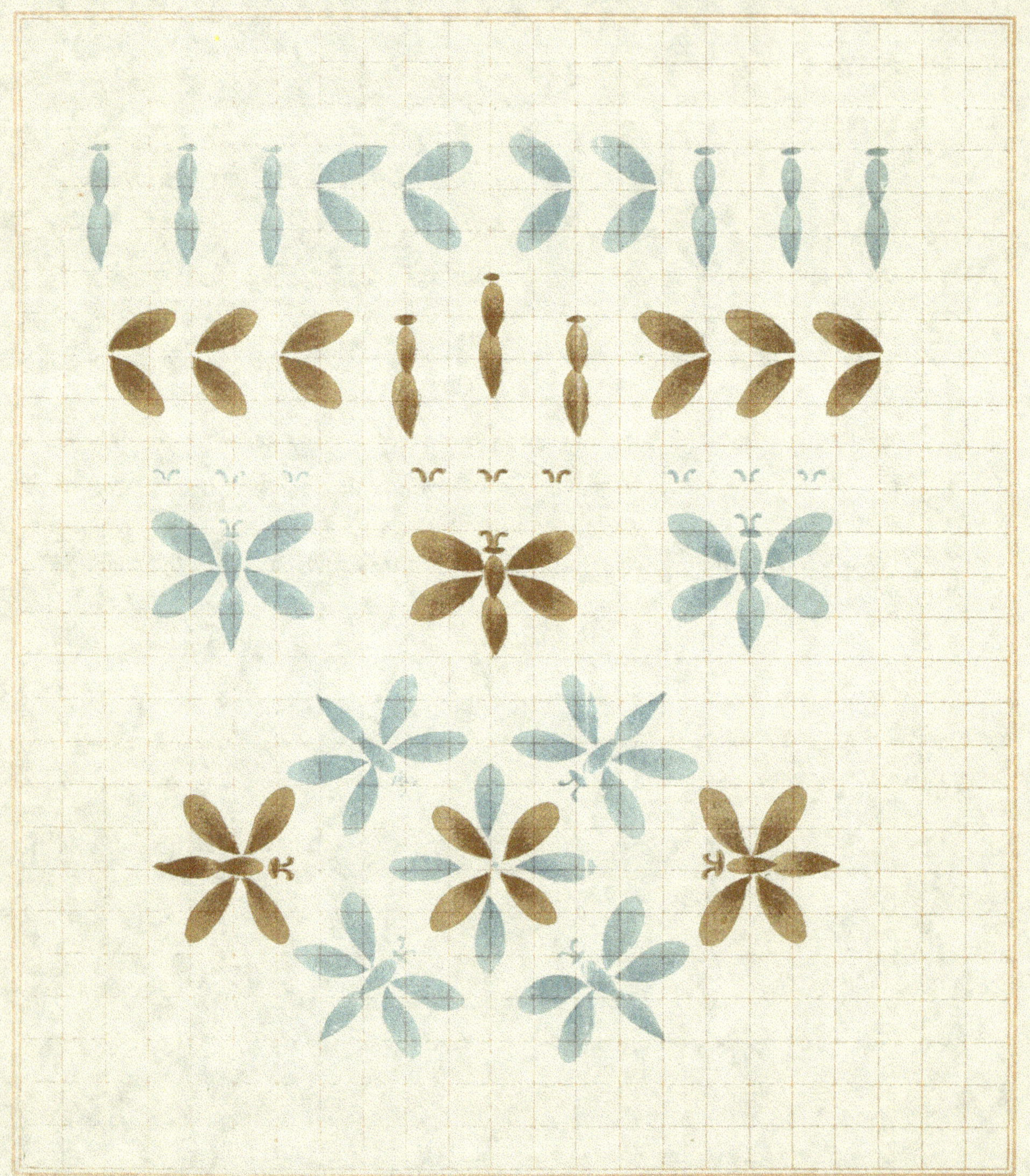

**LESSON 13.**

The bodies of the Butterflies are made by two touches with the brush reversed, the upper one, half the brush only, and the heads by just touching the paper with the point.

For the wings, point the brush towards the body.

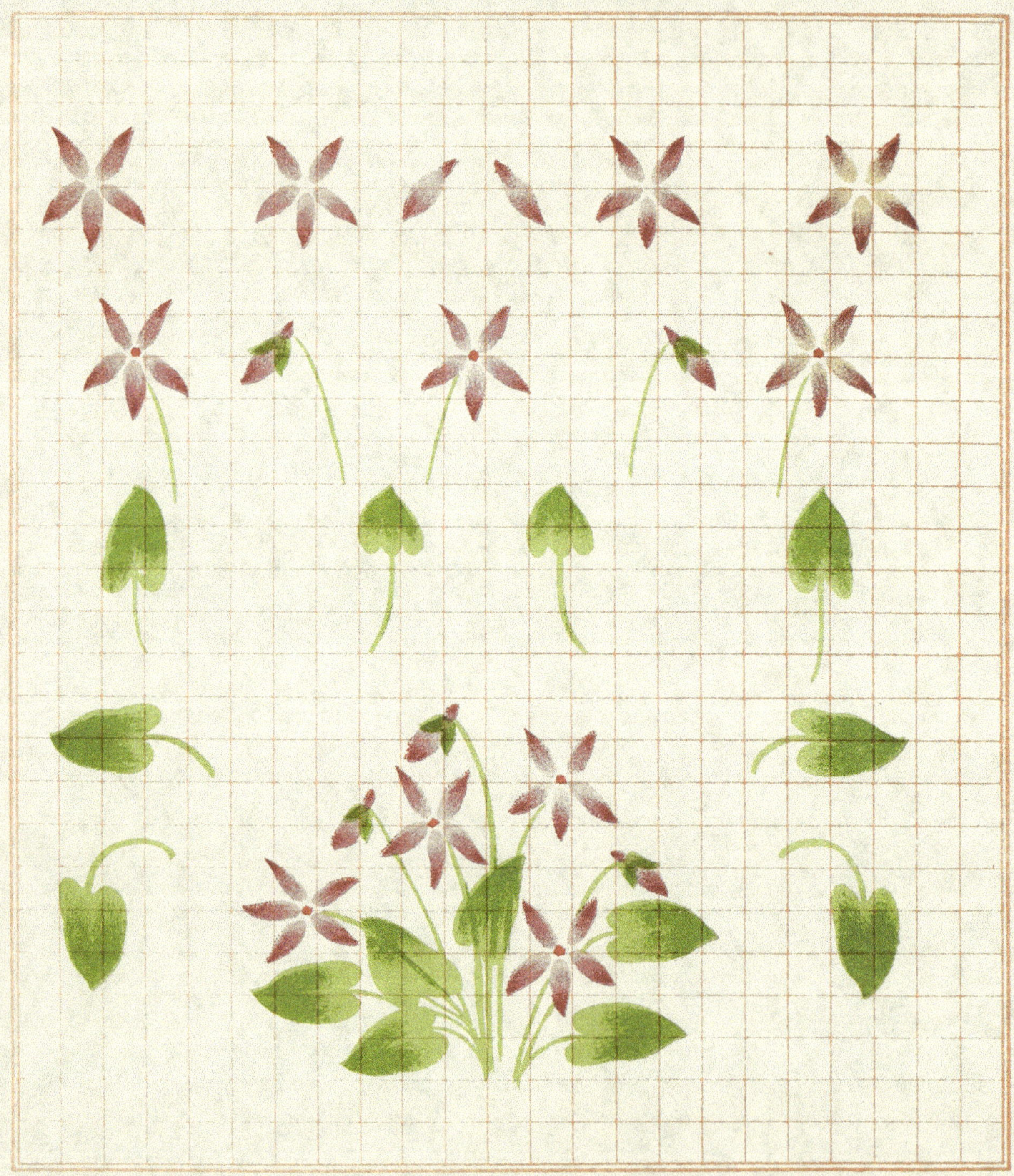

**LESSON 14.**

The touches should be made without pressing the brush down.

Make first, the two petals at the top, on each side of the line, then the centre petal at the bottom, and lastly, the remaining two, one on each side.

The leaves are made as in the Dahlia, but the last two Brush-forms with the brush in the same position, pointing upwards, so as to form the lobes of the leaves.

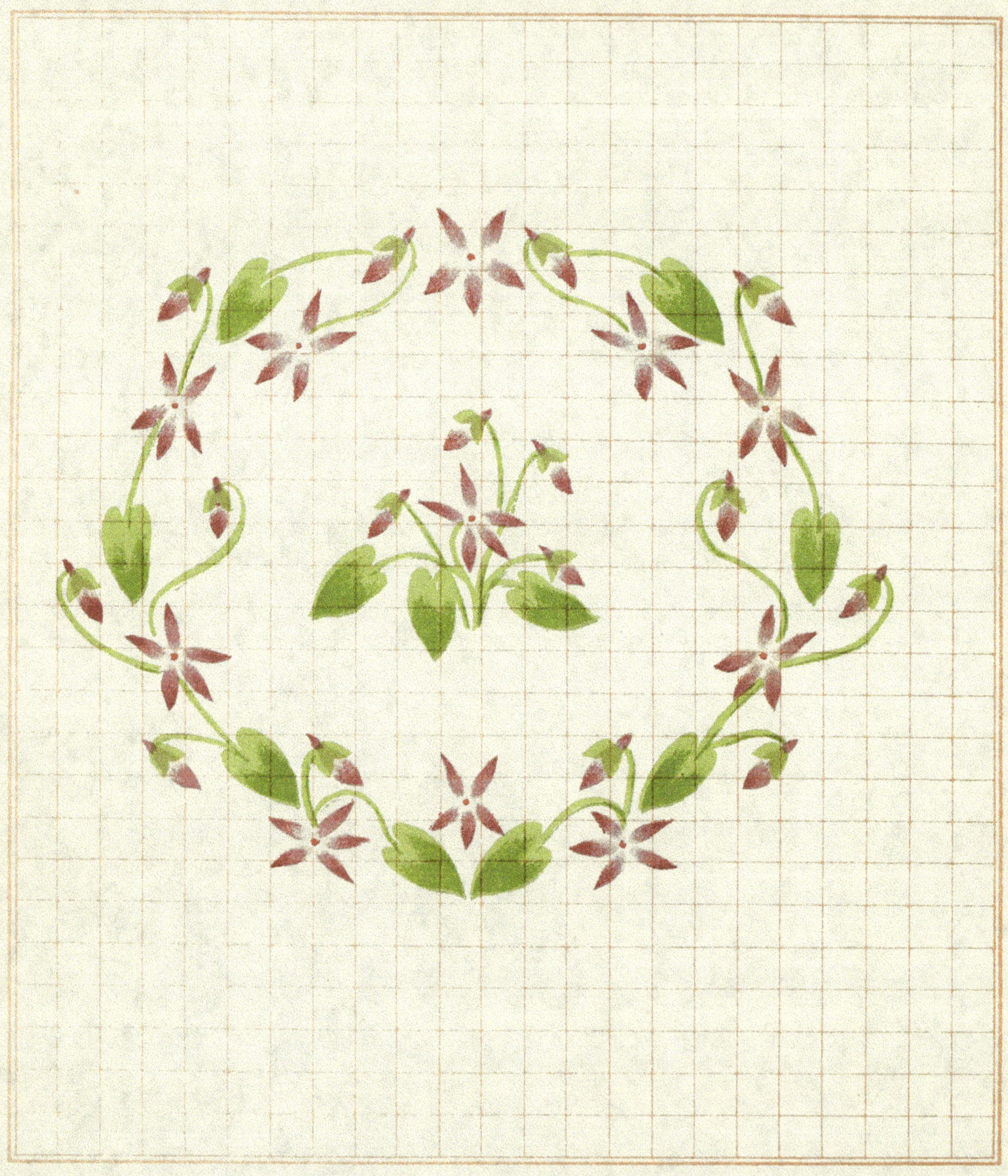

**LESSON 16.**

The Laburnum is made with two overlapping Brush-forms, beginning with one on the vertical line. The calyx by two touches of green.

For the spray, make the stalk, and place a flower on each side alternately, then on one side place a second row, where the flowers are not sufficiently thick.

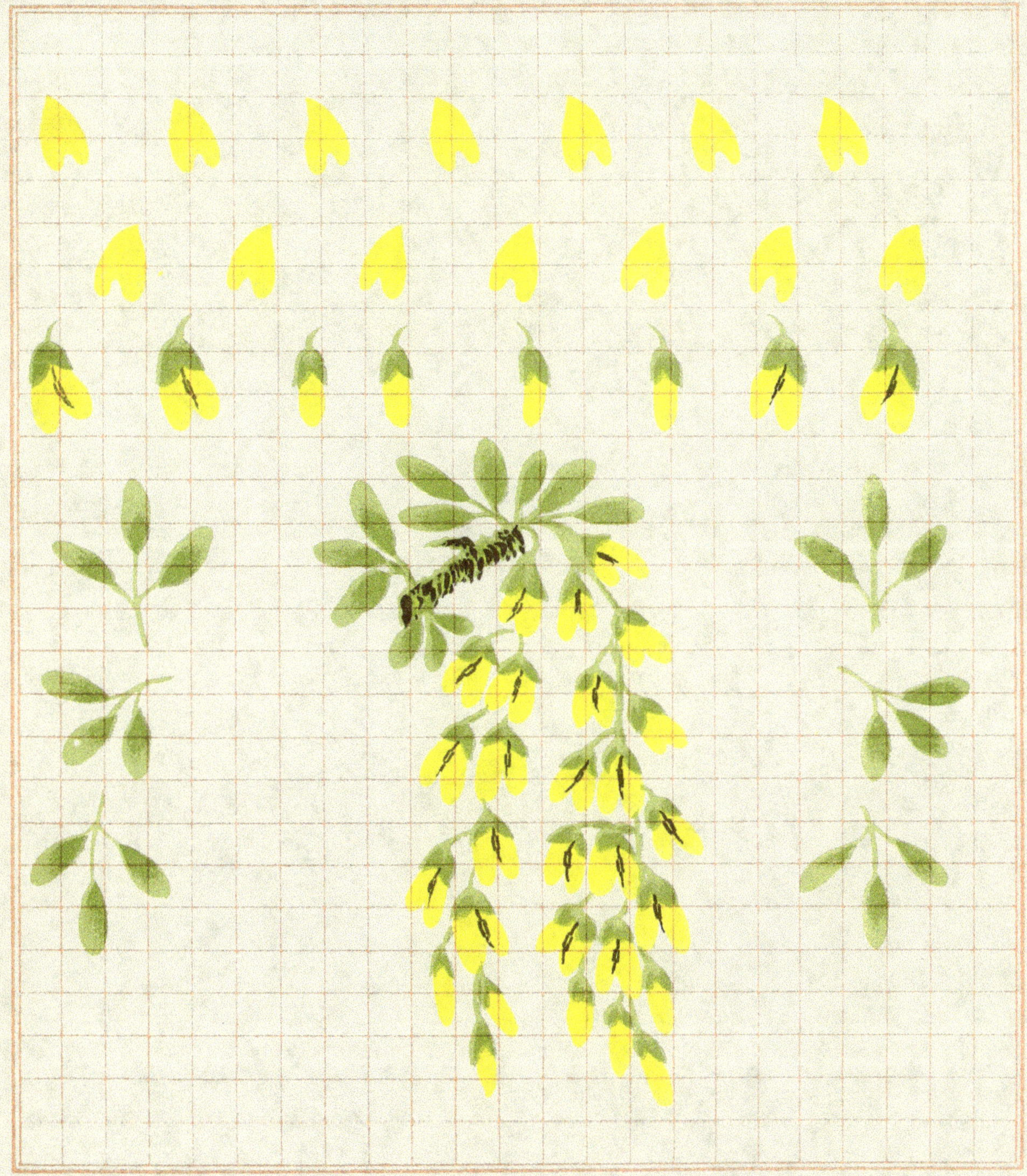

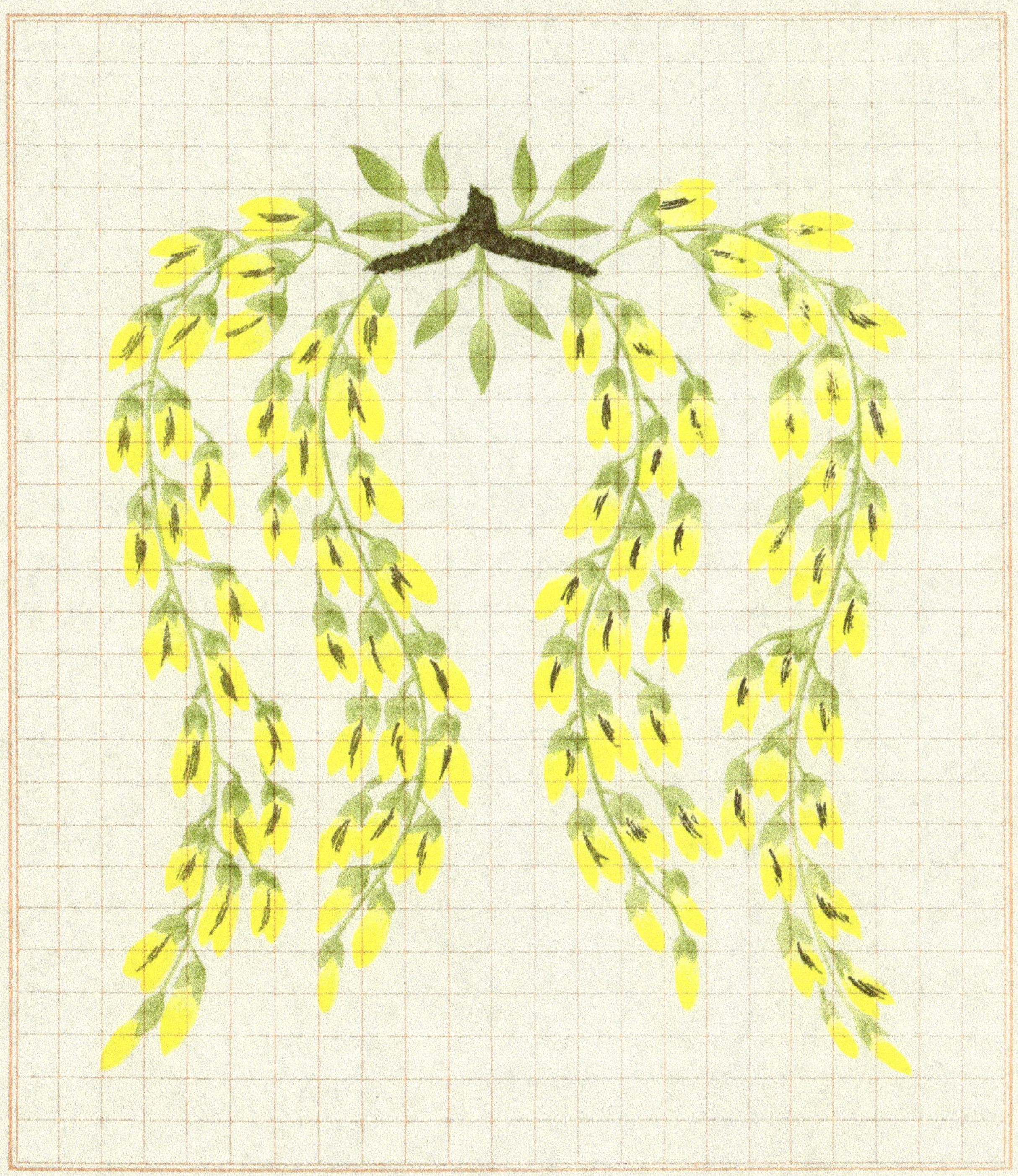

**LESSON 18.**

The hares are made with one vertical Brush-form, adding the ea/s, back legs, and tail with a touch of the brush point.

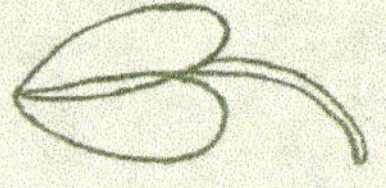 In the leaves, two Brush-forms overlap, the point of the brush being towards the right or left for each pair. A single Brush-form represents a fore-shortened leaf in front.

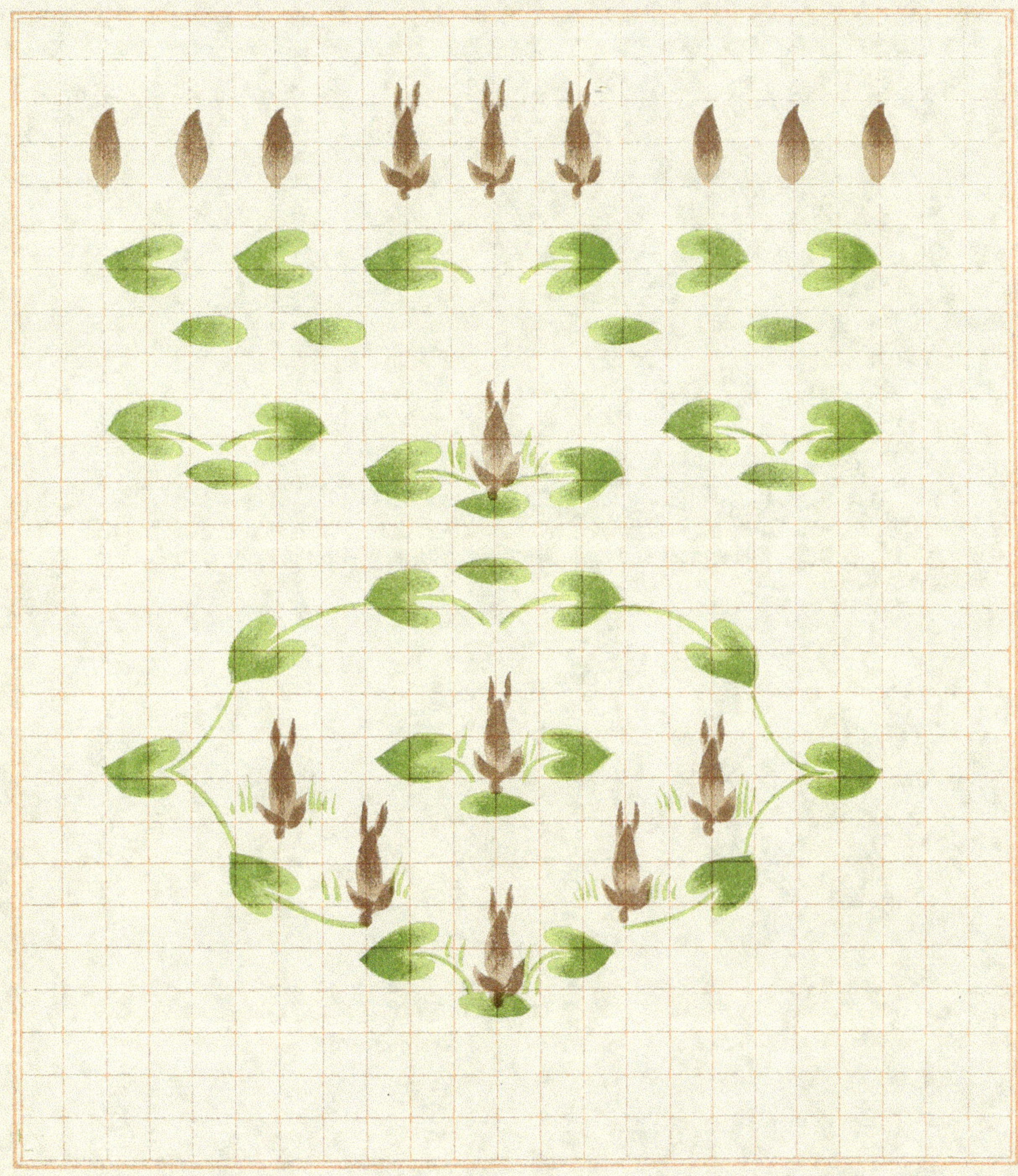

## LESSON 19.

The body of the duckling is made with two horizontal Brush-forms overlapping; the head as in the chicken (Lesson 12).

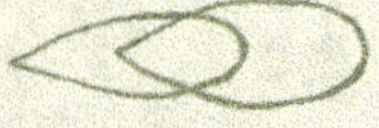 The grass and pond are merely strokes with the brush point.

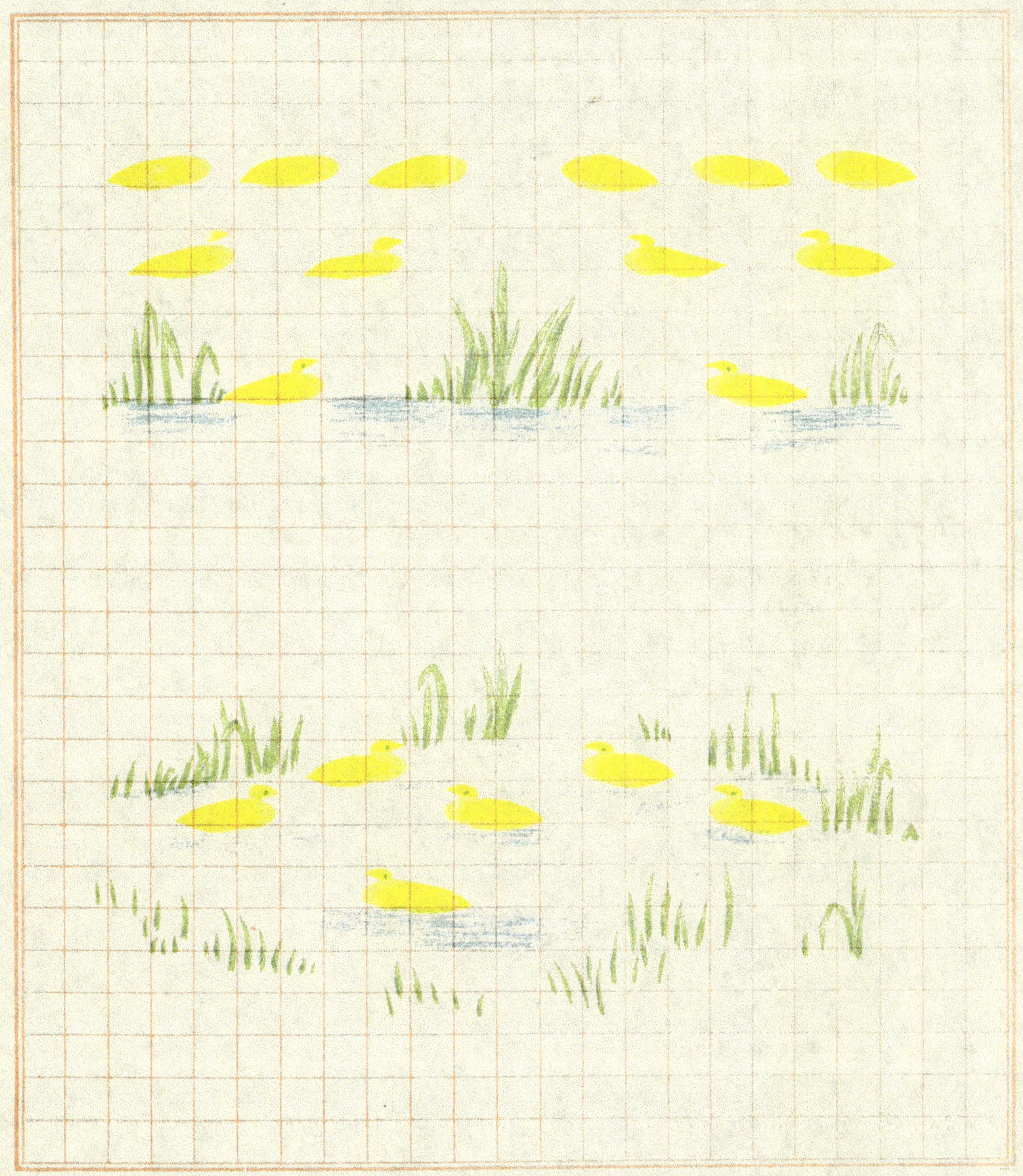

**LESSON 20.**

In the pointed ivy leaves, the vertical form should be made first. Next, the two forms pointing downwards, overlapping the first form at the base to make them shorter, and finally, the two pointing sideways of medium length.

The elliptical leaves are made like the leaves in Lesson 8, and the berries with the point of the brush.

Note the two different kinds of leaves and difference of growth.

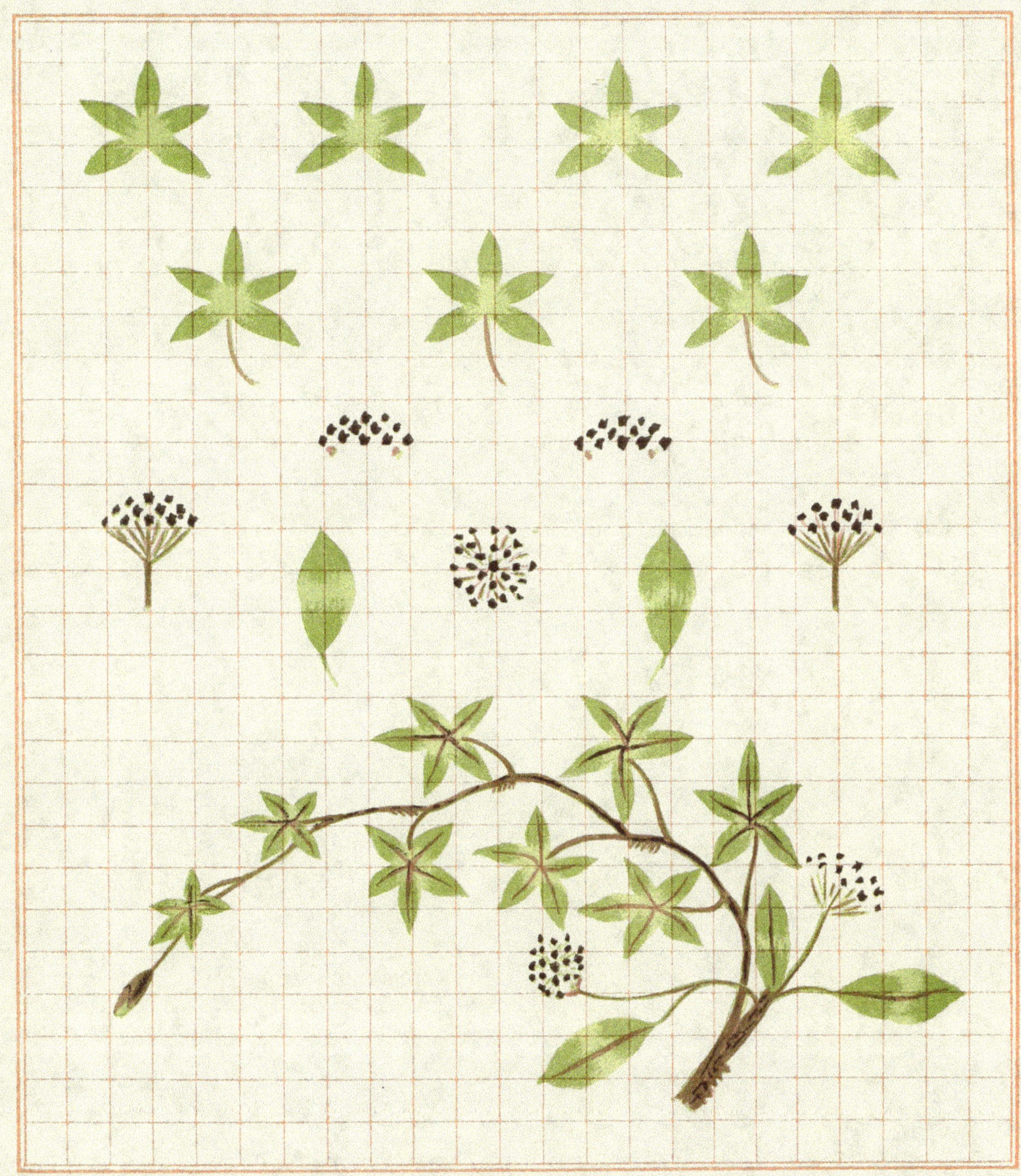

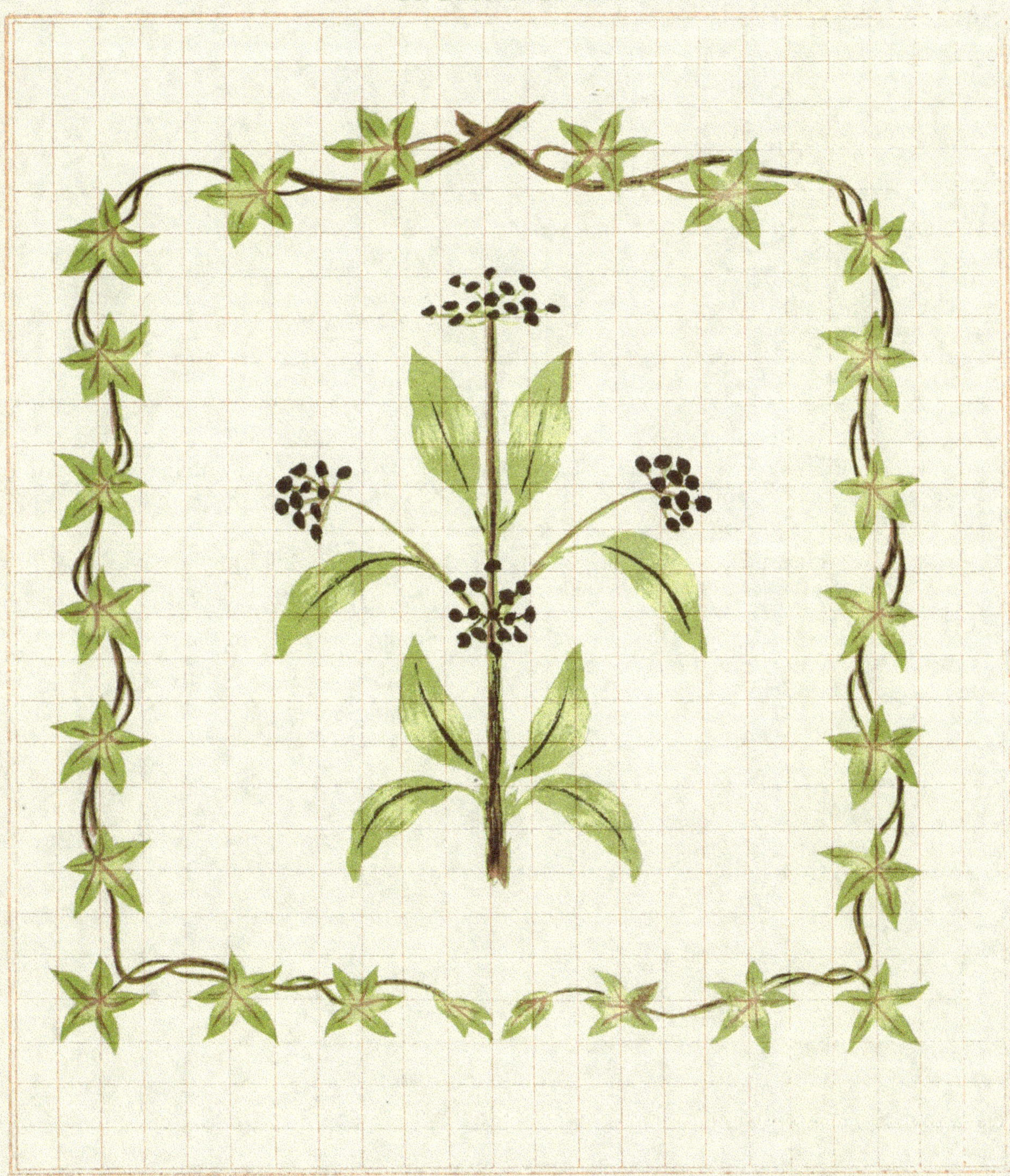

**LESSON 22.**

The berries of the mountain ash are formed by making a little ring with the brush point, leaving a tiny spot of white in the centre.

The arrangement of the branches may be dictated by beginning with the highest row of four berries on the corners of two chequers, and adding the rest in rows above and below.

The leaves are simple Brush-forms arranged on the chequers, but the stalk should be curved, to prevent the appearance of stiffness.

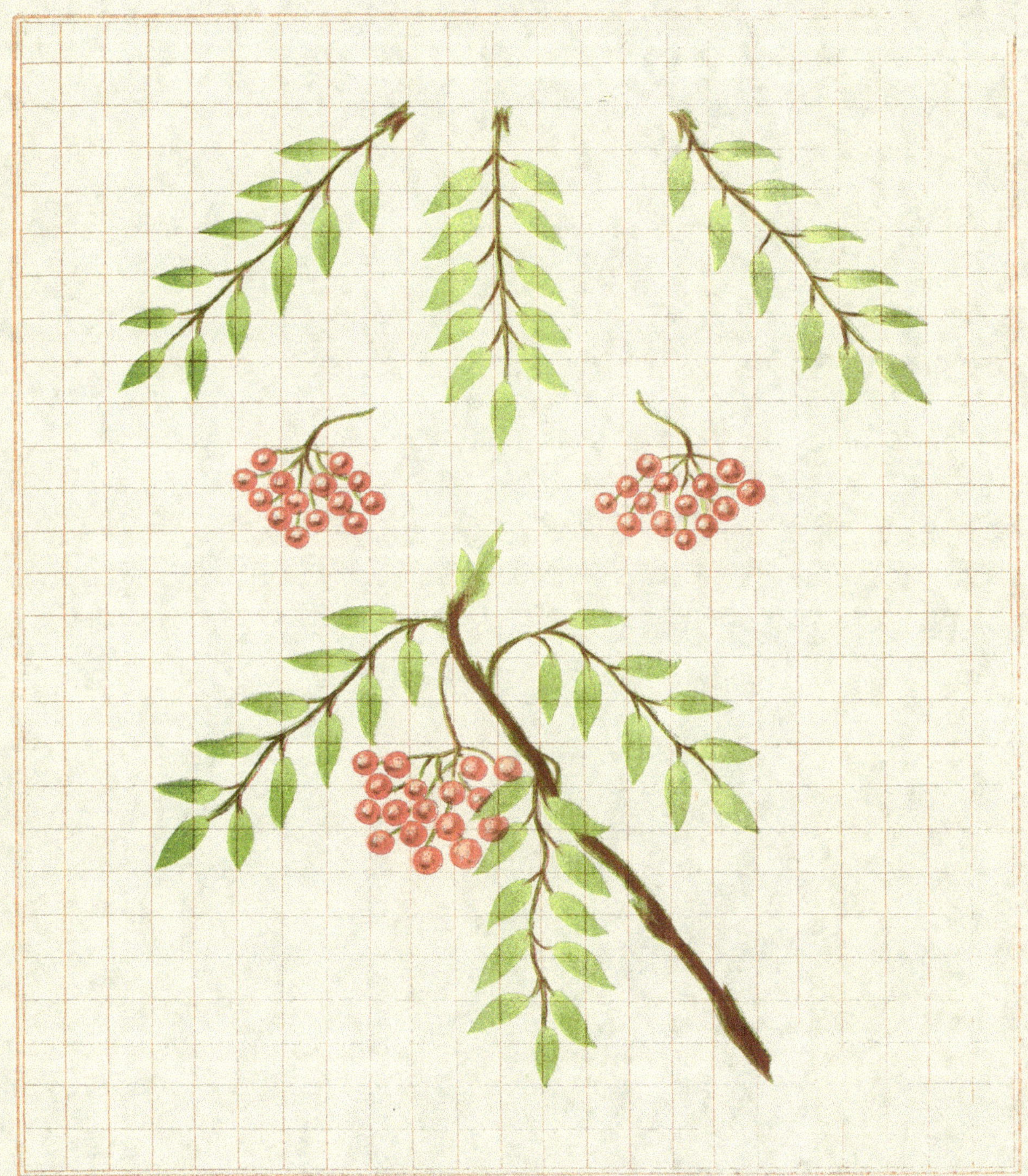

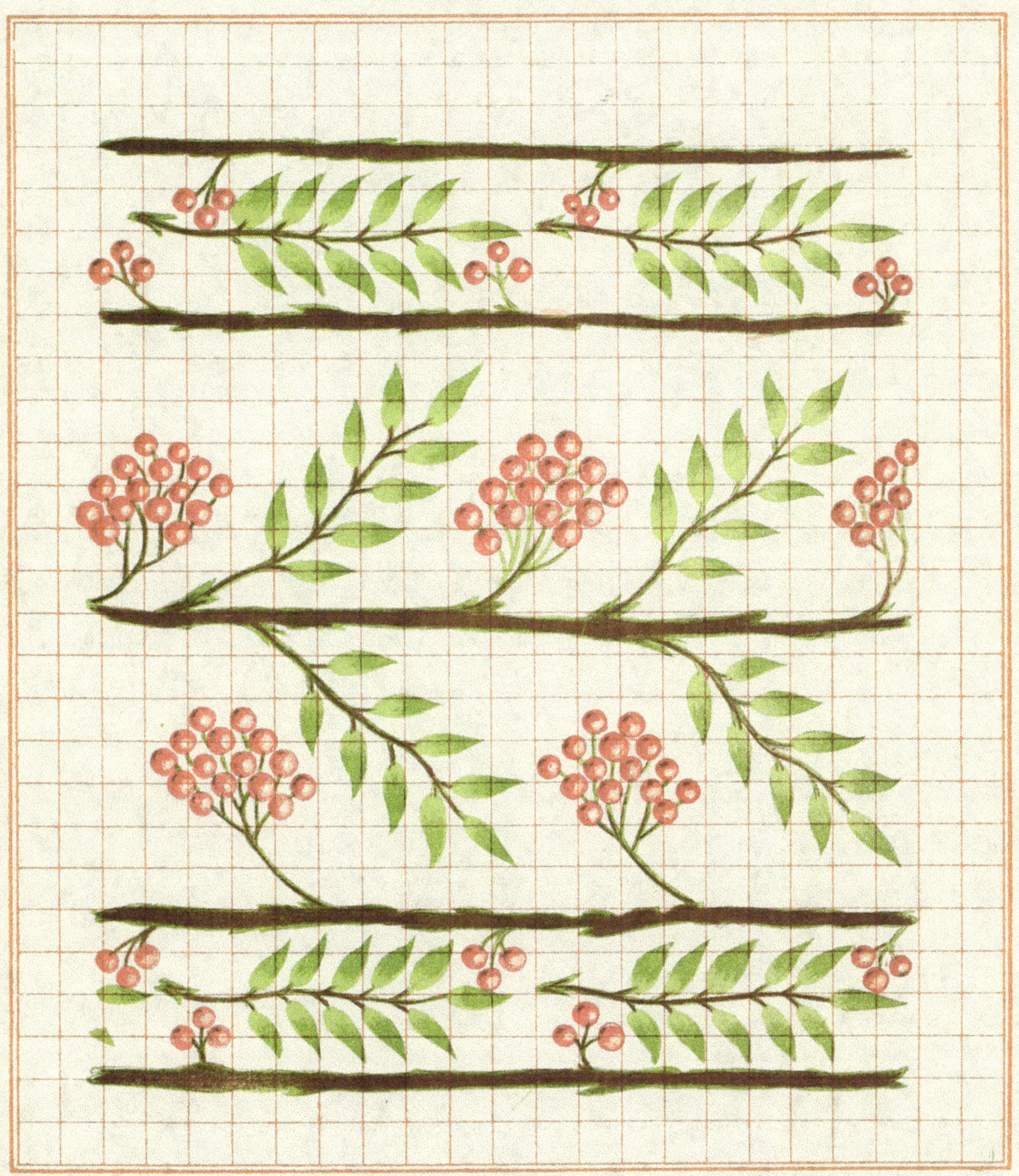

**LESSON 24.**

The stem of the corn should be made first, afterwards adding touches on each side with the brush point.

The mice are simple Brush forms, with the addition of touches for ears, legs and tail.

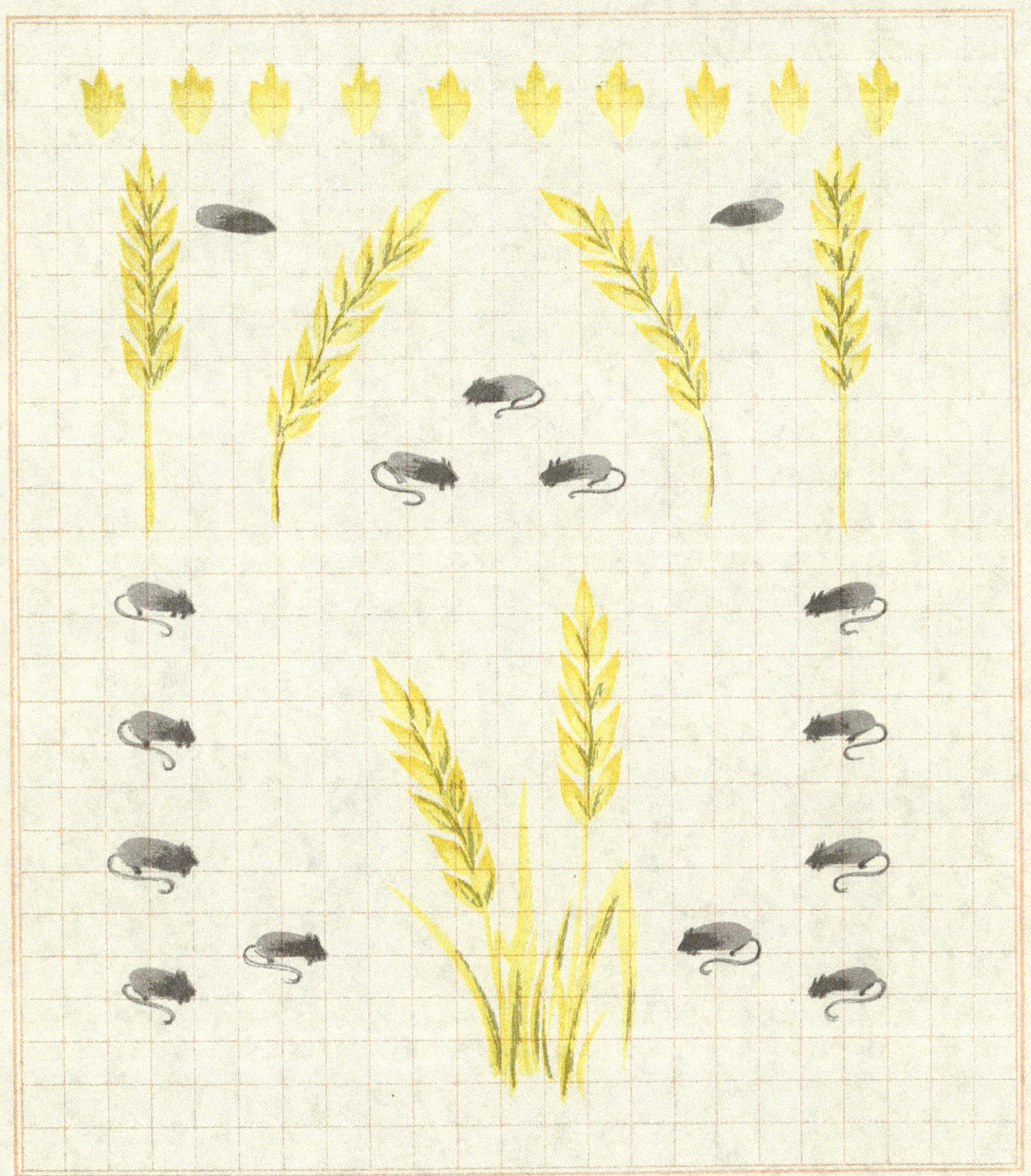

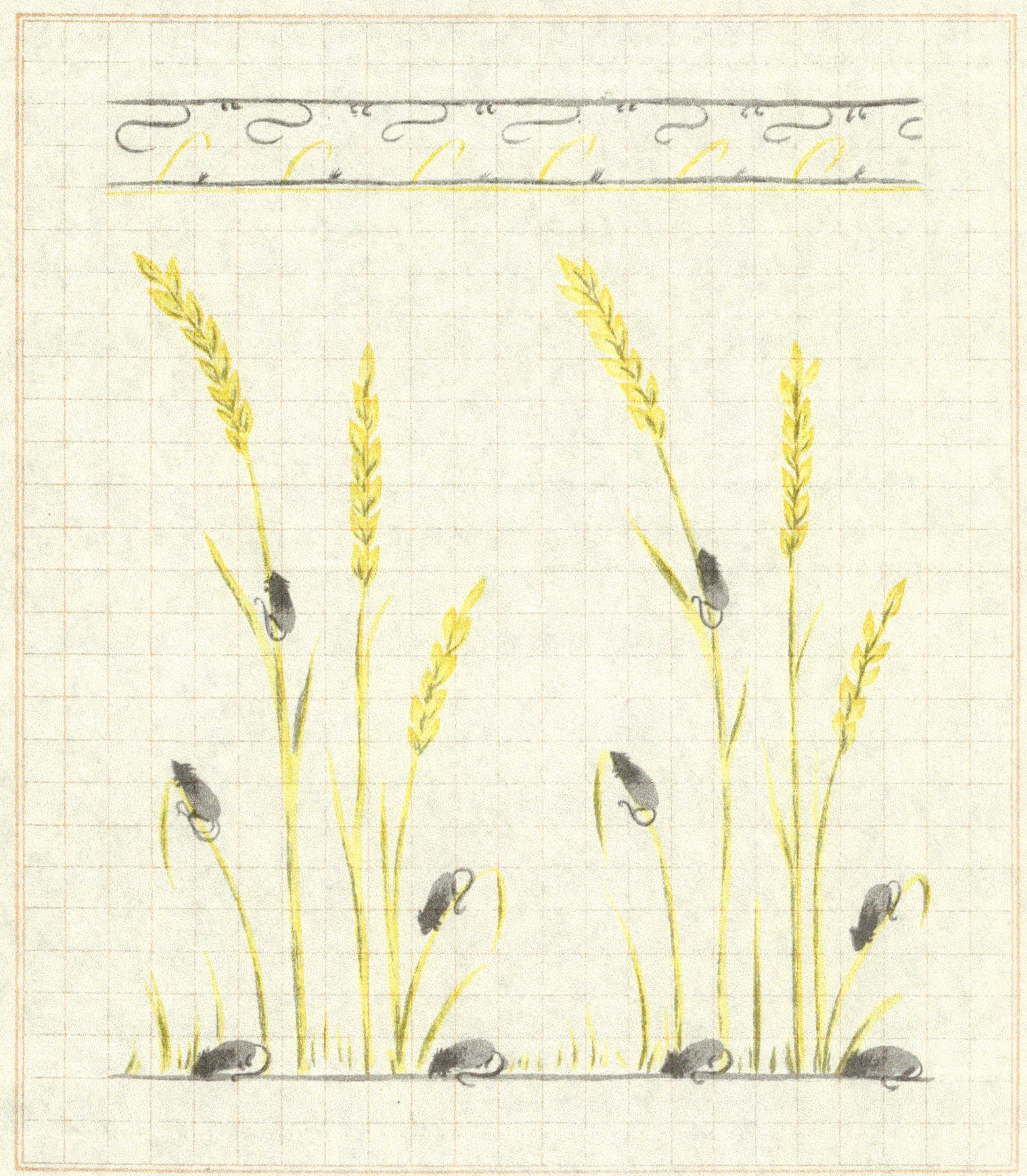

## LESSON 26.

The flowers of the anemone are made in the same manner as those in Lesson 8, the centre, however, being smaller, and filled with little curves, as in the French anemone.

The leaves are a combination of the touches used in the leaves of Lesson 10; the three long points should be made first.

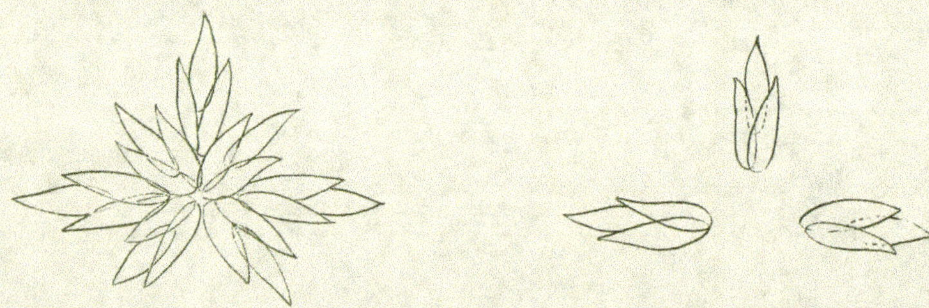

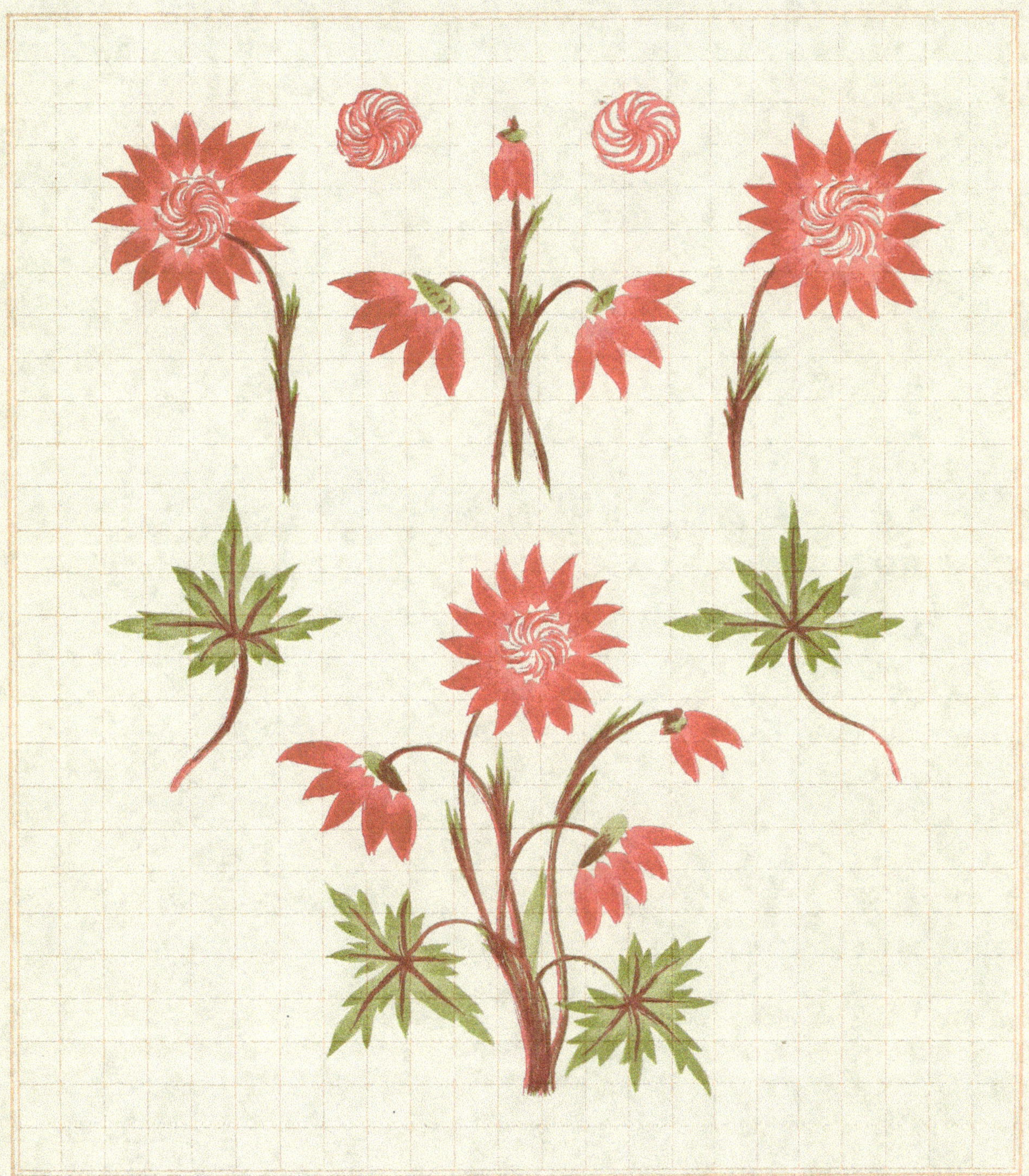

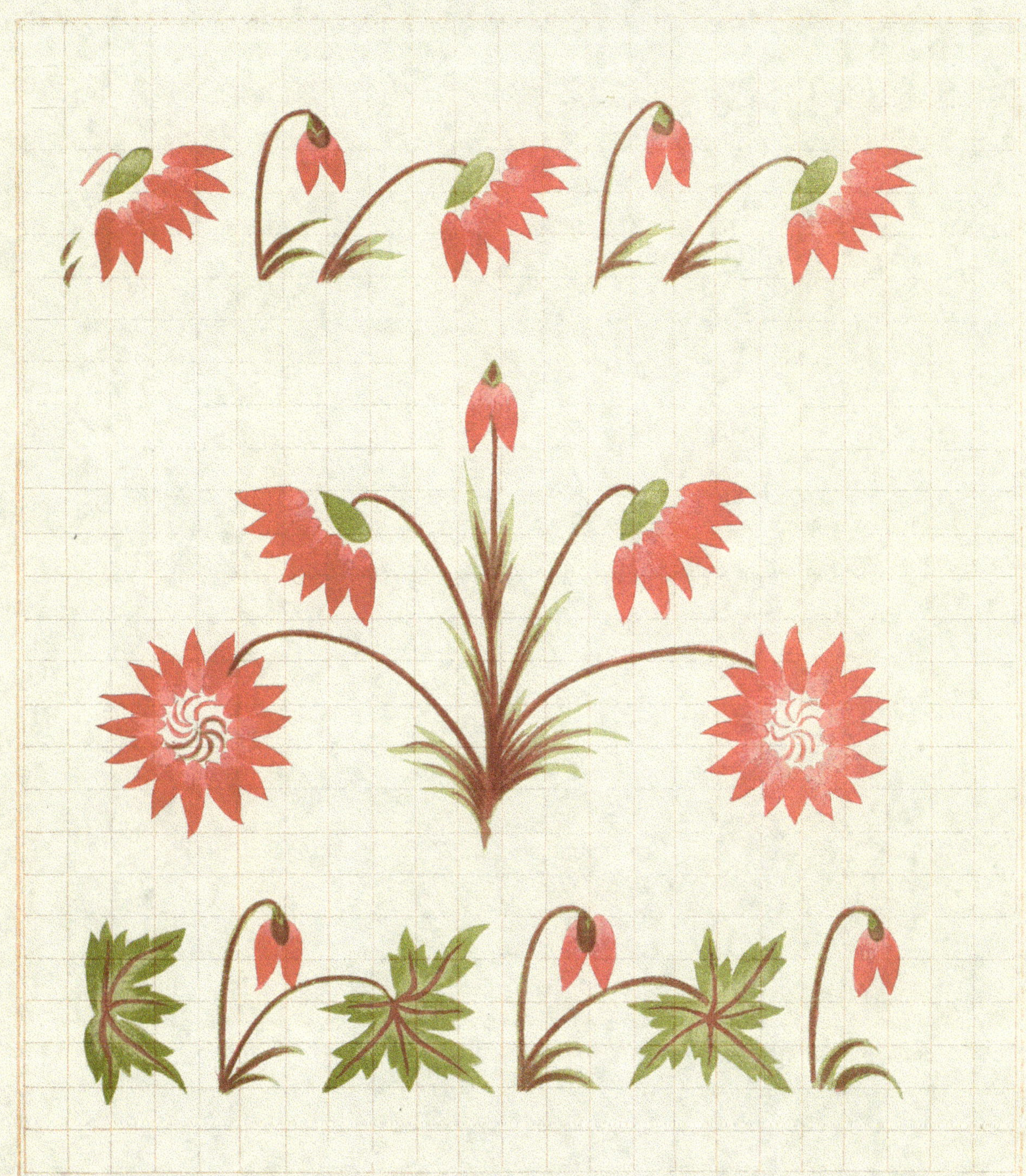

**LESSON 28.**

The bodies of the larger storks are made like those of the ducklings (Lesson 19), but in an oblique position.

The tops of the bulrushes like the violet petals (Lesson 14).

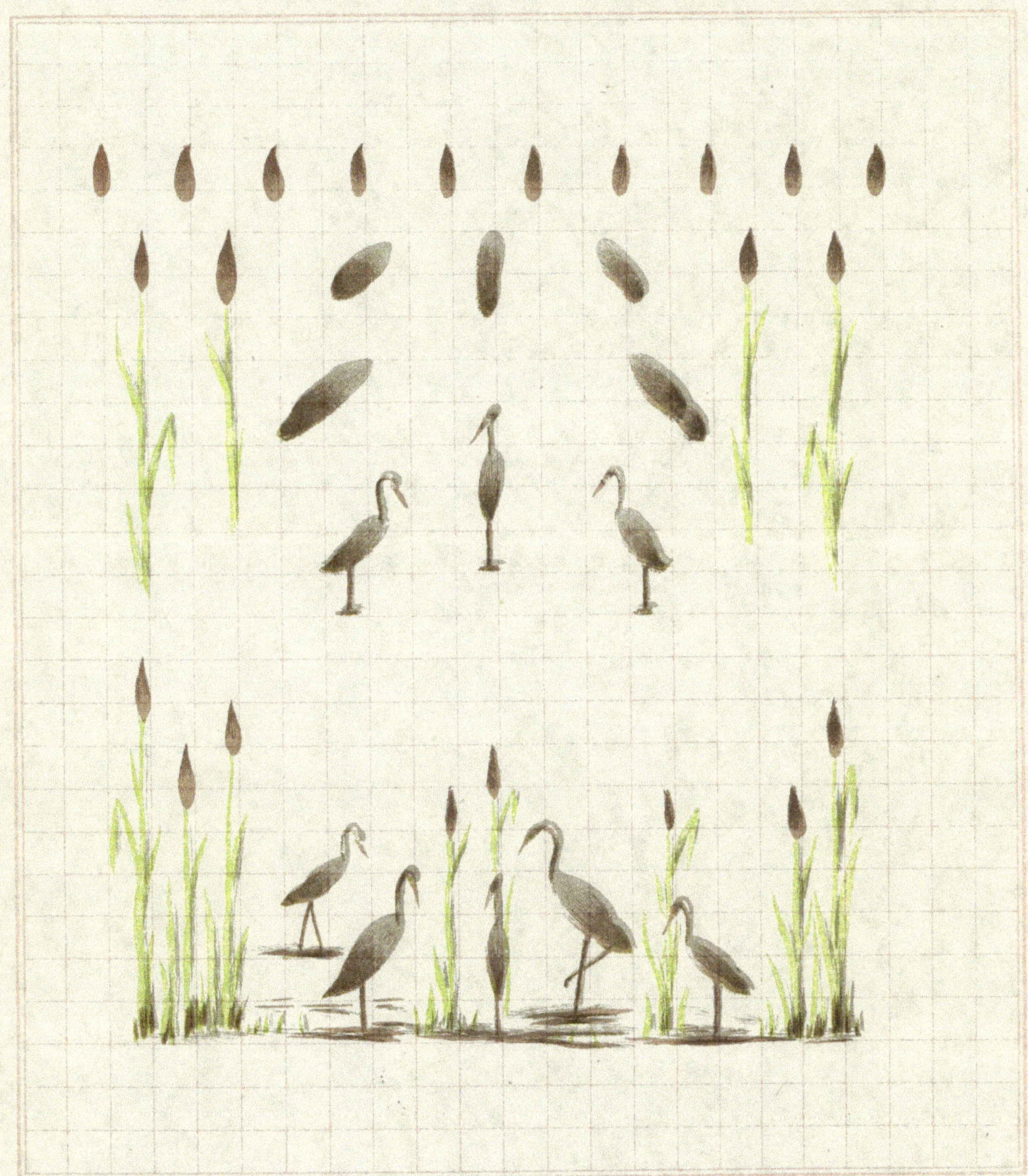

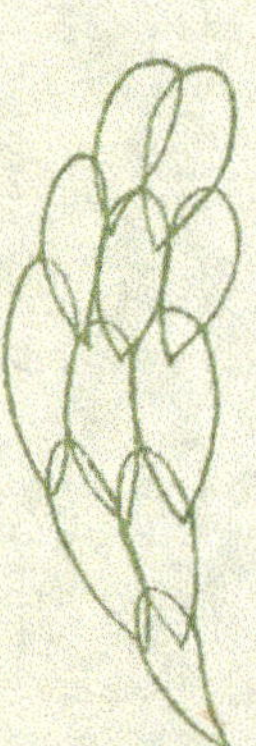

### LESSON 29.

The petals of the primrose should be made separately, at first, of two overlapping Brush-forms (see plate). Make a pair of petals at the top on each side of the centre line, then the lowest petal, and lastly, the remaining two, one on each side.

By placing the petals closer to the centre, they will just touch each other, as in the finished flower.

A succession of Brush-forms placed side by side, give the rough appearance peculiar to primrose leaves.

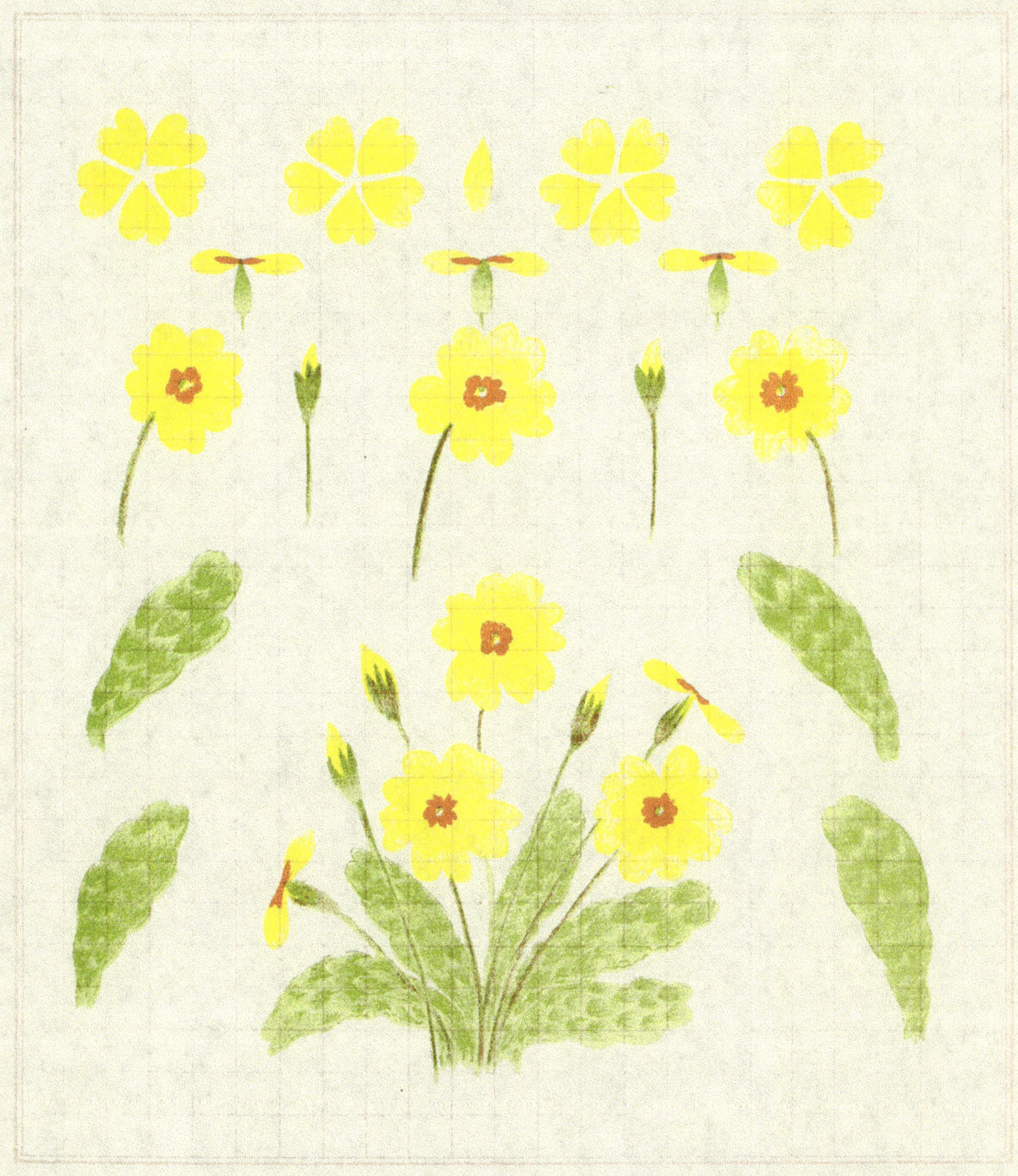

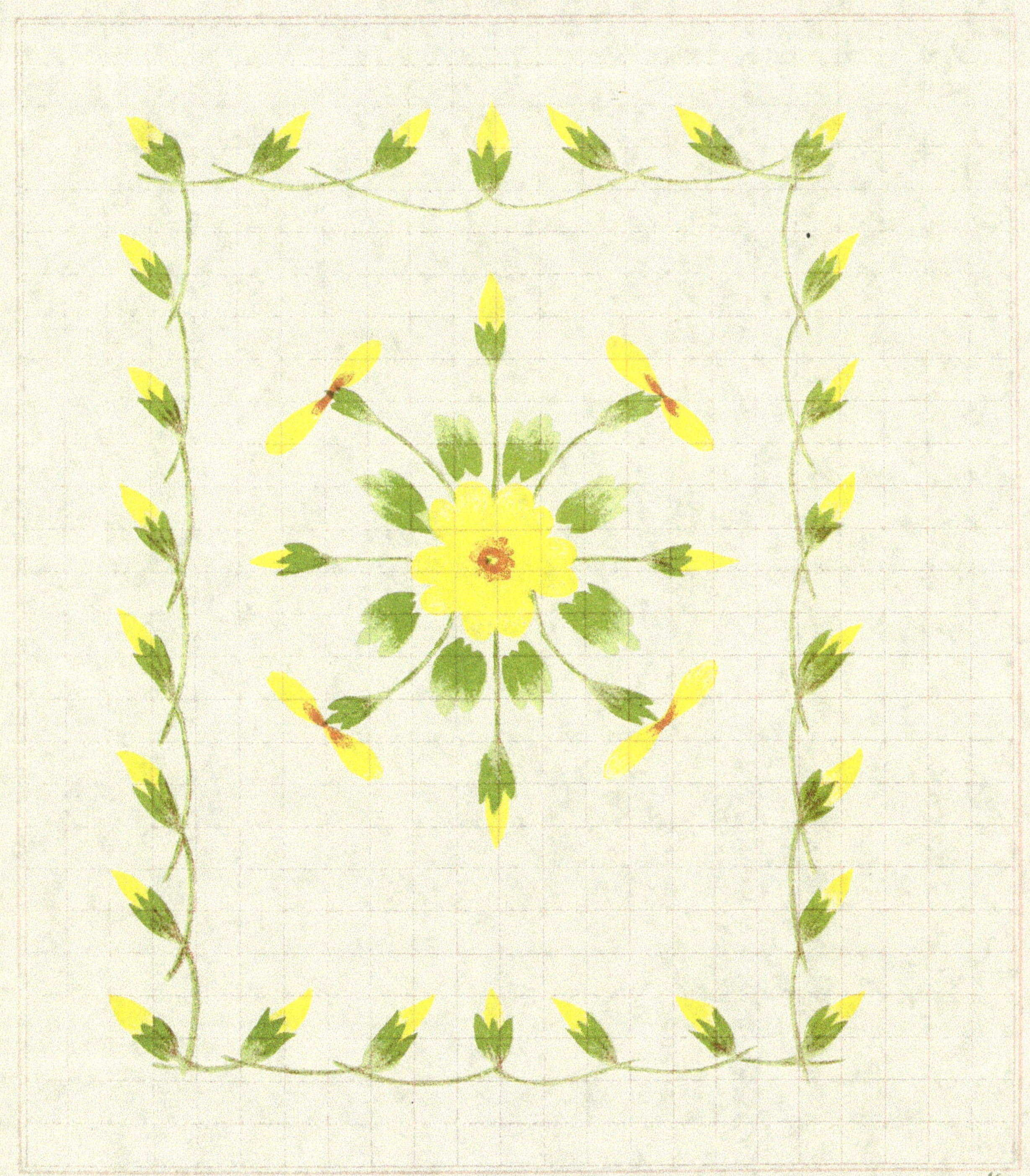